GETTING BACK
ON TOP

THE UNCENSORED GUIDE TO SEX, DATING, AND RELATIONSHIPS AFTER DIVORCE

BY

SUCH A PLEASURE
TO MEET YOU!

IAN OLIVER

IAN

© 2014

You can find more information and contact the author at:
greatlifeafterdivorce@yahoo.com
www.2ndchanceatromance.com
https://www.facebook.com/2ndChanceRomance

DEDICATION

BEFORE WE JUMP HEADLONG INTO THIS INCREDIBLY JUICY AND important jungle of human relations, I would like to dedicate this book to my mother. From the earliest age I can remember, she has been an inspiration to me as well as to many people in her life. Her determined and upstanding approach to all things in life combined with an unequivocal moral and ethical standing, real concern and support for her family and friends and a true passion for life has been a major driver and support in my life. Thank you Mom for everything!

TABLE OF CONTENTS

FOREWORD

GETTING BACK ON TOP IS THE ULTIMATE RESOURCE FOR A HEALTHY divorce, dating, relationships, and sex. In his book, Ian masterfully tackles the challenges of love, romance, and commitment in our current fast-paced, high-tech world, and he offers crucial strategies to achieve interpersonal success in all relationships.

After divorce, how should you ideally prepare to start dating? What's the importance of psychological insight and self-awareness? Stylistically written like a personal, intimate conversation, *Getting Back on Top* is actually a comprehensive guidebook that offers you all the knowledge and tools necessary to transition back into dating and relationships. As a reader you will feel as if you are listening to your dearest friend, gaining wisdom from a respected parent or mentor, hearing candid feedback from a sibling, and gathering psychological recommendations from a mental health professional.

What are the best resources available and the best methods to meet appropriate mates? How should you approach issues of sex, commitment, and blended families? Ian shares a wealth of information from years of personal and professional experience that, if applied, will save you a tremendous amount of time, energy, and money, not to mention heartache.

What are the potential joys and common pitfalls in the dating world? And, ultimately, how will you keep your new relationships personally rewarding and sexually thrilling? Ian grants you permission to be fulfilled in your relationships and emphasizes the importance of knowing yourself completely. He understands the significance of healing and insight, and the value of honesty and direct communication. Comfortably and candidly addressing practical facts about sex for both men and women, Ian provides specific recommendations for counseling, online dating, and matchmaking, as well as romantic hotspots and travel getaways. You may refer to his 10 Commandments as a quick reference for a foolproof method of relationship success.

Between the lines, this book supports a concept that most individuals either don't understand, or choose not to acknowledge. Healthy relationships require work. You need to be willing to devote time and energy to continued personal growth and to the process of relating. You need to prioritize honest communication and sexual intimacy. However, Ian's use of humor, wit, and storytelling will have you embracing this work so that it feels more akin to an exciting journey and novel adventure.

Written specifically for divorced individuals, *Getting Back on Top* is a masterpiece for any adult. This book offers educational information and pearls of experiential wisdom beneficial not only for divorced singles returning to the dating market but also for divorcers/divorcees attempting to achieve healthy separation, for married couples and significant partners desiring to keep the spark in their relationship, and for sexually active individuals striving to attain ultimately gratifying sex and sustained romantic intimacy. So start reading, and get back on top today!

—*Dr. Martha Koo, leading Los Angeles psychiatrist*

INTRODUCTION

ON HALLOWEEN EVE 2005, AS I SIGNED MY DIVORCE PAPERS, I had no idea what lay ahead. I knew for starters that I wanted a better, future romantic relationship than the 13-year one that had just ended (which included 10 years of marriage), but I had no inkling about the extraordinary journey that was about to start.

Before I got divorced, I never would have dreamed I would someday experience crazy and unpredictable dating escapades, surprisingly aggressive and sexual women, online dating sites, life coaches and shrinks, dating and matchmaking services, trysts, one-night stands, one- to six-month relationships, longer-term relationships, friends-with-benefits dating strategy, going away strategies, or blended-family issues (i.e., my dating partner's kids' relationship with my kids, etc.). And so much more that I would discover and explore!

Getting Back on Top is a specific and detailed account of my experiences and learning as both a divorced, single man in his 40s and 50s (a man who was and is profoundly dedicated to learning about sex, dating, relationships, and overall communication between the sexes) and as an adviser to many couples, guiding them through their divorces and into the single world over the past 10 years. Over that time, I have dedicated a large portion of my personal and professional time to this effort. That time and effort, combined with a little luck and intelligence, have yielded great results that I now share with you so you can create your own success.

How deep is my experience in this area? I have gone on more than 400 dates and experienced six post-divorce relationships. In addition, I have worked professionally with many couples through their divorces.

Using my skills developed over a successful 28-year financial career, I am systematic, analytical, creative, and adventurous with my research and information accumulation. This approach has yielded a treasure trove of valuable information for both sides of the dating fence that I share in *Getting Back on Top*. Now you have a no-holds-barred, candid, practical approach to sex, relationships and dating after divorce, gleaned from my divorce and post-divorce learning experiences and integrated with all of my research and discovery from my many years of working professionally with divorcing couples.

You may be asking, "How does a financial career qualify you as an expert on post-divorce sex, dating, and relationships?" As a financial adviser and money manager, I counseled numerous married couples, and of course a certain percentage of those couples ended up in divorce. Initially, my advice was exclusively limited to financial matters. But then about 10 years ago, my divorcing clients began looking to me as an adviser in non-financial matters. They had seen me navigate my own and others' post-divorce dating lives, and they wanted to know how they could manage their transition and immersion into their single lives.

Every divorced couple I have advised and guided has managed to remain cordial and non-adversarial. All of them have minimized the lawyers' involvement, and each person has transitioned successfully into a vibrant singles life. Several are now happily remarried. So this evolution in my professional life of turning toward more guidance in sex, dating, and relationship issues has also given me tremendous practical insights into the relationship between the sexes.

You also might be wondering how I am qualified since I have no psychology degrees. Well, I have dedicated a large portion of my life to this effort since 2001, and I have carefully documented and analyzed every aspect of the experience. Essentially, I have completed a practical, clinical PhD in the lab of human experience. Furthermore, in consultation with several psychiatrists and psychologists, I have engaged in intensive examination and review of the ideas, strategies, and processes that I have identified and developed. As I mentioned above, my professional financial work naturally led me into advising many couples on their lives as couples and then after their divorces on their lives as single people, and that has yielded tremendous practical knowledge, experience, and insight. I have also included some success stories to *show* you how these methods work, rather than just telling you about them.

Though *Getting Back on Top* is somewhat geared toward men, and obviously written by a man (so inevitably presented through a male lens), I believe that women will find this book extremely helpful—but for different reasons. While men will learn more about specific actions to take, thought processes, and strategies to adopt for themselves, women will become better able to understand the male mentality and why men act the way they do. So while this book is prescriptive for men, it is equally illustrative and illuminating for women.

To help you navigate these changes in your life, I have written this book in as close to a logical chronological order of the overall process as possible. I started with the prologue about the pre-breakup/pre-divorce considerations and continued through the divorce process to how and when to start dating. From there, I explore:

- dating and sex strategies
- sex itself in great detail

- kid issues
- how to deal with STDs, birth control, and abortion
- payments and financial issues
- online dating sites and matchmaking services
- shrinks and life coaches
- the most common types of people you will encounter
- developing serious relationships
- the "exclusive" decision
- a raft of incredible dating stories
- the absolute 10 Commandments of Sex, Dating, and Relationships that you must uphold

Many newly single people and professionals in the field have confirmed that the information you are about to receive is totally unknown to most divorced, new singles. I believe you will find it immensely helpful in minimizing frustration and unpleasant experiences (and can save a huge amount of time and money!).

My overarching goal is to offer you a comprehensive, ongoing relationship-enhancing process, of which this book is a part.

I will continue to offer assistance and guidance in addition to this book through my website, seminars, and follow-up books, as well as through my relationship coaching. If you would like more information and assistance, you can contact me for advice, counsel, feedback, and more by emailing me at **greatlifeafterdivorce@yahoo.com** and/ or by visiting my website at www.2ndchanceatromance.com.

ACKNOWLEDGMENTS

I WOULD LIKE TO PROFOUNDLY AND GRATEFULLY ACKNOWLEDGE the following people who were instrumental in supporting me in general and in my effort to create this book:

Martha Koo, Lily Shariat, Michelle Saul, Richard Levak, Helen Segal, Mecca Dyes, Emilee Moeller, Sydney LeBlanc, Nina Babaie, Tim Vandehey, Jon Larson, David Mattana, Steve Samuel, Kia Sinay, Suzy Nece, Janis Spindel, Dina Moskowitz, and Wendy Porcelli.

PROLOGUE: TO LEAVE OR NOT TO LEAVE. MANAGING THE DIVORCE PROCESS (READ THIS EVEN IF YOU ARE ALREADY DIVORCED!)

IF YOU ARE READING THIS BOOK, YOU'RE PROBABLY ALREADY separated or divorced. Even so, you can still benefit from this chapter. Go through it carefully, completing the steps and processes and checking your "emotional self" each step along the way. Regardless of your current marital status, the information in this chapter is vital to establishing a clean and firm emotional foundation after the divorce so you can form healthy long-term relationships. In addition, these tips may help you handle any potential breakups in the future as well as other relationship issues.

The ideas and suggestions in this chapter are also designed to help those of you that did not have a cordial divorce and currently have an unpleasant or adversarial relationship with your ex. Work to implement these ideas and strategies even if your divorce is final.

You have a good chance of creating a cordial, amicable, and cooperative post-divorce relationship with your ex by using the techniques and strategies in this chapter. It is **so** worth it. I can't overstate how important it is to the health of your life, your children, and your future romantic relationships to achieve a friendly tenor with your ex. Be patient and unrelenting in the pursuit of a kinder, gentler rapport with your ex. Sometimes it might take months or years (or it may never happen), but it is worth giving it your all. It doesn't take much effort to continually offer the olive branch, and you never know when your efforts will register and finally be received. I have seen several situations in which, out of the blue, even after many years of horrible relations, a wonderful thawing and cordiality take over.

Be creative as you use this chapter. Think about changing some of the terms of your agreement if that will help. (See the disclaimer at the beginning of this book and remember to consult your attorney in legal matters concerning your divorce and separation.) Really think out of the box on this one. This step is vitally important to your long-term emotional and relationship health.

Finally, this chapter will be of immense value to you if any future relationship starts to go bad. You'll have the tools, as well as the specifics, for protecting and saving an existing relationship or, if necessary, properly guiding a failed relationship through the best possible transition. All of the ideas apply whether or not you are married; it is just less messy legally if you are not! This chapter is your guide to evaluating and handling the possible unwind of any romantic relationship in your life.

So let's begin.

***

You are or were unhappy in your marriage and have been for a long time. You hardly have sex, if ever, and when you do, it doesn't ring your bell anymore. Day-to-day obligations and mundane activities have crowded out your relationship.

Does this describe you? Well, you are not alone. Several studies show that more than 70 percent of married couples are dissatisfied overall with their marriage, that more than 75 percent of married couples admit to having sex two times or less a month, and that more than 70 percent of married couples admit that sex has become boring or worse. So what should you do? What *can* you do?

One thing you **should not do** is just sit there and do nothing.

Accepting an unhappy, dissatisfying status quo is unacceptable. You know by now that life is short. You deserve a vibrant and stimulating romantic relationship. You also know that being alone is far better than being in an energy-sucking, dismal, sexless relationship.

First, though, do all you can before you end the relationship so you know you tried everything to make it work. After all, over the years you have invested a lot of time and energy into this relationship. And divorce is hell, even under the best of circumstances.

The following steps can make a huge difference in your relationship, either way it goes.

1. **Talk** to your partner during a time of low stress when you both are not distracted or in a rush. The timing of when you sit down to talk to your partner is absolutely critical. After a long day's work? Not a good idea. Instead, try a Saturday morning after the two of you have worked out and the afternoon is free. Or perhaps on a Sunday after you've had a nice brunch. Make

sure logistically that you don't have any time limitations and can talk freely to each other for as long as you want.

2. Share what your concerns are and what you want; include specifics. Listen to your partner's wants and needs and constructive criticisms. Make sure you are both listening and hearing each other. Don't talk over each other. Don't talk over each other! This is not a typo—the point is worth repeating. People do it all the time, and when you are both talking, neither of you can hear the other.

3. I know what I'm about to insist that you do may seem awkward, but it is a time-tested, important technique: Each of you repeat back to the other exactly what you heard your partner say. You don't need to do this for everything, but make sure you do it for **all** the important points. It feels clumsy and silly at first, but it really works. **Try it!**

   And this applies to all relationships, all the time. It is a great technique to prevent misunderstandings and fights in the first place, and a way to slow down the pace of the discussion and make sure you both are listening.

4. Go to couples counseling. Give it at least five to seven sessions to see some progress. Work hard at it. Make sure the therapist is very talented and a good fit for the two of you (see Chapter 4, Life Coaches and Shrinks: Essential Partners). If you are already divorced or separated and not on good terms, you should go to couples counseling to try to make it amicable or at least peaceful. Couples counseling creates a safe and calm environment with well-guided discussion. I find couples counseling to be wonderfully binary in that it either leads to

great progress and improvement in the relationship or clearly highlights that the relationship should end.

WHEN YOU MAKE THE DECISION TO LEAVE

After you have tried everything and the relationship is still not working, then decide to end it—but hold your horses! To create an optimal separation, you have some critically important planning and work to do before you share your decision with your partner.

1. For your financial protection, make sure you know:
    -   All the account numbers and locations of all of your bank and investment accounts and insurance policies
    -   Where all your estate-planning documents are.
    -   The names of your attorneys and CPAs.

    Even if things unravel and your partner tries to move accounts or money, you will have a trail to follow. These days hiding assets is very difficult, as there is an electronic trail of everything.

2. Talk about the possibility of a breakup and divorce beforehand on several occasions over several weeks. Get your partner to the point that the subject is not a shocker or taboo. That way, when you sit down at a carefully selected, calm, and open-ended time, the news won't be a surprise, or at least it will be less jarring than if you did it cold, with no warning signals.

    Remember, the highest priority as you go through the divorce/breakup process is to try to keep it cordial and non-adversarial. This is never easy. The one on the receiving end of the breakup often feels rejected and spurned, especially given that most relationships often have so much history and emotionality, including resentment and anger.

Get your partner to buy into the concept of the breakup so it feels to your partner that it was a ***joint*** decision. If you can achieve this, it will bring tremendously more peace and civility to the breakup process. It is worth putting in a lot of time to achieve this—even if it takes months.

I readily concede that getting your partner to buy into the breakup is extremely hard. The best chance you have at actually achieving this is to encourage a lot of dialogue within the context of a calm environment. And what does that mean? Again, the timing and setting of when and how you discuss this issue is absolutely critical. Try not to talk at the end of a long day or when either of you is tired. I know I've already mentioned this, but it bears repeating because I've seen so many people choose the wrong time. Most divorce processes unravel because of emotions run amuck, with bitterness and anger driving retributive behavior.

So keep trying to talk calmly with each other and to come to a conceptual agreement on how you will handle the divorce. With this general agreement as your foundation, you have a chance at keeping the whole process cordial.

3. Once you have your partner's buy-in or even reluctant acceptance, then jointly discuss the process of the divorce. Try to get an agreement on mediation. See if you can work out the details together, keeping lawyers out as much as possible.

They will draw up the final documents, but hopefully that will be the extent of it. Even the best lawyers are inclined to be adversarial, stirring the pot and ratcheting up the conflict.

4. ***Control*** the process. ***Control*** the lawyers. How do you do this? Have as many discussions and meetings that you can *without* the lawyers. When you do work with them, be direct and precise with them. Ask your lawyers to give you weekly updates on their hours and spending. They will resist, but insist. Take the lead and be as present and thoughtful as you can be in this horribly wrenching and unpleasant process.

5. Discuss what attorney you will each hire. Once you get your partner's buy-in to a more friendly process of mediation or the two of you doing it alone, that's the time to discuss your attorney choices. Again, this keeps what would otherwise be a very divisive and adversarial part of the process more cordial and cooperative. Why? Because as soon as either of you talks to an attorney, that attorney is disqualified from potentially working with your partner. I've seen highly adversarial couples interview a ton of attorneys, thereby eliminating many of the top lawyers that their partner could choose from because of potential conflict of interest and attorney-client privileged information!

Avoid this debacle by having a specific discussion about how the two of you will approach selecting your attorneys, and then coordinate your efforts, discuss your meetings with prospective lawyers, and try to jointly agree on both lawyers. In the end, it benefits you when the two lawyers have a good rapport and working relationship.

I fully recognize that achieving a cordial separation, breakup, and divorce is not always possible. Sometimes the emotions and hurt are just too much, and bitterness and retributive behavior dominate. What I am providing you with here are tips and techniques to keep yours cordial and friendly, whenever possible. I want you to try everything humanly possible to stay away from that horrendous divorce you hear about. When all has gone according to plan, you will both feel as though it was a joint decision; lawyers will be chosen; assets will be split; and alimony, child support, and custody will be agreed on together and mostly peacefully. This outcome is so much better for you, the kids, and your friends and family. It will save you both, as well as the kids, a huge amount of time, stress, and money, so do everything you can to achieve it.

6. Manage the process. Keeping things anywhere close to cordial is *very* hard to do, and emotions can easily spiral out of control. If you're having a bad session with your soon-to-be ex, end it and schedule another one. Cut your losses; don't allow the process to unravel. Remember that this time and this process are arguably the most difficult and emotional things in life, so you will have setbacks even in the most amicable of breakups. Remember this and reset. Don't allow the situation to spiral downward.

   Take a break, take a deep breath, and meet again the next day, fresh and resolved to keeping it friendly. Whenever things deteriorate, and they absolutely will, one of you has to be the bigger person and pull the both of you out of the spiral. And it is OK if it is always you. Be above it, keep the long term in mind, and *always* remember that in a contentious, combative divorce, ONLY the lawyers win—EVERYONE else loses.

7. Force yourself to compromise. This is one of the best secrets to keeping the process cordial. Give as much as you possibly can, within reason (but remember to take into consideration legal advice). Push yourself to the limit of what you can accept. You have to be just shy of creating hardship and lasting resentment for either of you.

8. Talk to your divorced friends in great detail. Try to grasp what you are facing and how difficult it is. Getting divorced or going through a significant breakup is one of those life experiences you cannot possibly understand until you have experienced it yourself, like being a parent or being pregnant. Nothing prepares you. But talking to those who have gone through it, survived, and then thrived can help you internalize at least some of the process. Talk to as many of them as possible, both men and women, as you will get very different perspectives from them. Talk to your psychologist/ psychiatrist and life coach, of course, as we discuss in Chapter 4. You can't talk or inquire too much about this process to try to prepare yourself.

The better you are able to manage the divorce process, the sooner you will be able to move on with your life and begin dating. This is, arguably, one of the most exciting and stimulating parts of your life! You will know yourself better than you ever have and will know what you want better than ever. You will be meeting sexy people and having great sex—and a lot of it, if you want! You will meet incredible people with whom you will have wonderful relationships, and hopefully you will find your ultimate relationship.

SPECIFIC RECOMMENDATIONS

Here are some time-tested specific recommendations to make your divorce easier (see the disclaimer at the beginning of this book):

1. Strongly consider lump-sum payments for child support and alimony. It cuts the cords of negative interactions, and you don't have to keep writing checks every month, reminding you of all the negatives. Get it behind you. The calculations are easy, so it can be easily accomplished if both parties are amenable. Of course, this can be done only if you have sufficient liquidity, but if you do, it is an absolute no brainer.

2. Separate as many of the jointly held assets as possible; try to own as little as possible jointly. Buy each other out and separate stock certificates, partnership interests, etc. Almost everything can be divided. Do it. You need to be as separate from your ex as possible. If you have kids, you will be connected through them for a long time, so it is even more important that you sever every other connection possible.

3. After the divorce, make sure that your ex does not create any new connections. For example, many ex-husbands call or email their ex-wives during their kid time asking for help or input. Don't—unless it's an emergency. This is your time, and you need to be in charge. Another common syndrome: One of the former spouses cancels her/his time with the kids at the

last minute or tries to cut back on some current time. When this happens, especially in the beginning, don't always be there to do the bailing out. Force him/her to get backup or change schedules. Though I know you would rather be with your kids than to have your ex hire a nanny to care for them, you need to train your ex to be responsible and committed to his/her time and that you are not the expected backup.

4. Don't go to the gym or grocery store that your ex goes to, and minimize common friends, events, and activities. You are ***divorced***, which means *separate*! Be that. It is absolutely critical that you reestablish your own new identity and life. Make it truly your own life. This seems obvious, but can be very hard. Even negative connections provide psychological comfort early on after a separation. Be tough on yourself, and try to minimize all contacts with your ex other than those that are absolutely necessary, like working out the kids' logistics or having co-parenting discussions on the phone. For those of you who have no kids together, the ideal goal is to eliminate all contact entirely.

5. Sit down together to tell the kids. This is usually the hardest moment in the divorce process. No parents ever want to cause their kids pain or grief, and you know this will. The good news is that the shock and initial fear and pain are usually transitory. Be unified with your soon-to-be ex in telling the kids that they will be fine, that they won't have to leave their school or home (only if that is the case, of course), that you are still and always will be a family, and that you both love them very much. Get counseling with a therapist who specializes in children and

who can coach you on exactly what to say and what words to use. Kids are much more resilient than we think, so believe it and trust in the process.

As it relates to the children, I can assure you that one of the silver linings of divorce is that, especially for men, you will become much better parents. You will have this specific time when you are "it," and you will embrace that special time. You will establish the rules and the feeling in the home and the priorities. Creating one-on-one alone time with one of your children and time with all the kids becomes so much easier than before when it was always a difficult juggle. Though co-parenting with your ex will be challenging, when you are at your home with the kids, it is just you, so there will be no disagreements on parenting style and decisions. Once you grow into having sole responsibility, you will find it so much easier and more peaceful.

6. Ask for support from your family and friends. If you don't ask, they might not know you want it. And you *do* want it; you need it even if you aren't aware that you do. Having people to talk to whom you love and who love you to talk to, in addition to your professional team, is extremely helpful in dealing with this terribly difficult time. Think about who you want to share the details of your divorce process with and enlist their support and interaction. Good friends and family want to help. Ask them to.

Remember, too, that your divorce is awkward and difficult for the friends you have in common with your ex. They don't want to take sides but might feel pressure to do so. Maybe your ex is pressuring them, or maybe their spouses have a different perspective on your future friendship. Talk to every friend that matters to you directly and explicitly about the situation and what you want from them in the future. Both of you will be relieved if you do, even if it means that with some you might have to put the friendship on hold for a while.

Here's an interesting and illustrative example from my divorce: My ex and I were both good friends with a married woman. My ex and this friend, we'll call her Robin, were closer than I was to Robin, and my ex just couldn't accept Robin being friends with me. So my ex gave Robin an ultimatum—she had to pick between us. When Robin told me about this, I said to her that she should stay friends with my ex, and I would just wait it out. Initially, Robin agreed, but then a few weeks later she told my ex that she wanted to be friends with both of us and that if she was truly being given an ultimatum, then she would have to pick me. She couldn't allow anyone to be so manipulative and controlling. Robin and I, eight years later, are still great friends, and my ex and Robin haven't spoken since that day. So sad and so avoidable. The moral of this story is to talk to your friends about the situation and avoid being so emotional and defensive. Each of our lives is a marathon, not a sprint, so don't burn bridges.

If you can achieve a reasonable amount of what I have described above, then you are ready to start the dating process! As you know, getting divorced is one of life's most difficult and stressful experiences, so cut yourself some slack. Give yourself plenty of time to adjust to your new life and circumstances and time to learn and grow from the experience. Handled properly, the divorce experience, though still a dark cloud in your life, is one with extraordinary silver linings.

SILVER LININGS

Let's discuss those silver linings briefly so you know what you can look forward to.

All of these surprising, positive outcomes are best achieved if you devote yourself to really reflecting on your failed relationship and your part in it, if you do the emotional work and allow for your emotional development, and if you seek professional help in navigating this journey.

- I have found that especially for dads, like me, divorce can help us become much more focused and dedicated parents. Since we become "it" during our kid time, we really have no choice but to take care of things and to focus on our kids. What a wonderful, unexpected consequence! I know for me that it helped change my whole approach to being a father. All of a sudden, it was so much easier to have quality time with my kids, and I always knew when I was on. In the conventional home, neither is clear, and as a result many great opportunities to spend time with the kids are lost. As you become a more dedicated and devoted parent, you inevitably also become more altruistic and less selfish as it relates to your children, the time you devote to them, and what you do for them.

- And there is a wonderful added benefit—you also become a more altruistic and giving person in general. Being a good parent helps make you a much better person in life, and divorce makes it more likely that you will become a better and more devoted parent.

- When you don't have the kids, you are FREE! What a glorious surprise this was. I had forgotten what it was like to be totally independent and free and single! I love this time. Sure I miss the kids, but I love this wonderful and meaningful time just for me. Within a conventional married home, it is so difficult to have any time alone, not to mention extended free time. You have the time and space to get to know yourself better, try new things in life, do so many of the things that you never seemed to have the time for. Now you do! It is a thrilling and exhilarating liberation.

- Another exciting silver lining is to be single at a more mature age. You are smarter, have more life experience, and understand so much more what you want and like than when you were last single, which for many of us was 10 to 20 years ago when we were in our 20s and 30s! When you are single in your 40s and 50s, it's a totally different ballgame, and, in my opinion, a much better one! Your confidence is so much greater, you know what you want and like, and you have a much wider range of people you can choose from in terms of age range, backgrounds, location, etc., that simply wasn't available in the past. These days, considerably older or younger partners for both men and women are commonplace. As we mature, we realize that what other people think is quite meaningless; we are increasingly able to not only understand and identify what we want, but we are also much better equipped to go after it.

- Divorce presents each of us with the opportunity to completely reinvent our lives and ourselves. What an extraordinary opportunity. Think about it. Within reason and given financial and children-related constraints, you can change everything— your activities, your hobbies and interests, your friends, your daily routines, your home and lifestyle, etc., etc. This new time in your life can be so exciting and exhilarating if you embrace it.

***

Good luck as you enter the next chapter of this book—and of your life! New and exciting experiences await you, including great new people, fantastic sex, stimulating weekend getaways and trips (see the section Going Away Together in Chapter 1), and fantastic new relationships, romantic and otherwise.

CHAPTER 1

━━━━━━━■━━━━━━━

DATING: HOW TO JUMP INTO THE POOL AND NOT SINK

So you are in divorce proceedings, and the process feels interminable, despite everything you do to end it quickly. Your soon-to-be ex is dragging it out, keeping unhealthy connections, and finding every reason to dispute things or say no to even your simplest request.

So typical, so commonplace, so painful, and so exhausting.

And you are desperate for positive interaction with the opposite sex! What do you do?

If there is anything in this book that I am 100 percent certain of it is that you should wait at least <u>six months</u> after your separation before starting to date any real prospects. I know that this is *extremely* difficult to do, and I surely did not discover this on my own nor convince myself of its inherent advisability. I did, however, eventually realize its intrinsic wisdom.

Getting Back on Top Tip: *Get a Life Coach.* I strongly suggest that psychiatrists and life coaches to guide you through the pre-divorce, divorce, and dating phases are absolutely essential (see Chapter 4). I did that during my process, meeting with both my life coach and psychiatrist at least once a week, and I had many phone sessions when I was out of town to maintain the continuity of the dialogue and the momentum. They were incredibly important contributors to my self-discovery and learning and to my becoming truly ready to date in a healthy manner.

My life coach, Michelle Saul, who is extraordinarily gifted and dedicated to her profession, insisted that I wait at least six months to date after I was separated. I was shocked, dismayed, and extremely resistant because I so wanted to have new and positive interactions with women. But, after her insistent explanations, I agreed.

What did she say that convinced me to wait despite my keen desire to plunge into the dating scene?

She explained that I was by no means ready for any kind of relationship. I had not yet completed the self-examination, self-exploration, and reflection that are so necessary to the personal development I needed to become a better partner and increase the chances of not making the same mistakes again. She added that given the emotional vortex I was in after my divorce (as almost everyone is), I would just end up running away from any women who became interested because I was ill-equipped to handle complex romantic feelings. Dating would be so unfair to them, Michelle explained, because I would simply have a string of meaningless sexual interactions that risked hurting these women if they became attached.

Disappointingly for me, what Michelle said made total sense. One of her funny phrases was that dating too early would only encourage the "casserole patrol," and I would soon have to turn them away!

I realized that dating so soon, too soon, would be an act of great selfishness. So, despite my strong desire to date, I began the six-month countdown.

The good news is that during this waiting period, you can start to reorganize your life and plan your initial dating approach. You can explore the learning process, self-development, and discovery that are so important to your success. This period of no dating provides the space and time to look inward and really self-examine. Creating an active social life too early can be a narcotic that distracts you from doing the difficult—but essential—personal work and development. It can also dull your feelings and emotions, which you need to feel and work through.

So how can you best use this waiting period? Given the tremendous uprooting divorce causes, what you need to do initially is logistically create the foundation for your new life.

1. First, find a good place to live. Your home is very important. It doesn't need to be large or grand, but it must be comfortable and safe. It needs to be a place where you are comfortable having the kids over and a place where they want to be. Ideally, the residence should be centrally located, close to their friends or a place where their friends can come, too. It should be a place

that you make fully your own. Sometimes it's the little things that do that. You don't need to buy ALL new furniture, but do get rid of anything that reminds you of the marriage. Put up your favorite art pieces and photos. Buy a few knickknacks to warm up the place.

Even if you end up staying in the marital home, there are many ways to make it yours, several of which are not expensive. Of course, more extensive changes, like remodeling, will do the job, but you can also remake your home with selected room painting, new carpet, rearrangement of art and furniture, or some reasonably priced new art or accent pieces. These can make a huge change in the feel and flow of your home.

2. Next, establish your new single routines. That includes:

- Shopping for groceries (which is a good place to meet people)

- Working out at the gym (important for your physical and mental health and another good place to meet people), and going clothes shopping (it's important to look good as much of the time as possible since you can make that first impression only once!).

- Going out with single friends. Don't force yourself if you don't feel like going out, but try to venture out, even for a little while, a few times a week.

- Attending concerts, running or charity events, or lectures that interest you.

- Taking a course.

Social interaction will lift your spirits and provide opportunities to meet people. As much as possible, try to do all these life activities away from where your ex does them. Not only do you want to minimize the chances of running into him/her, but you also want to begin running in totally different circles. Start increasing your circle of single friends because chances are that while you were married, most of your friends were also married. Hanging out with other single people will not only provide you with welcome company but can also become a source of other single friends and potential introductions for dates. Also, these activities will help you realize that you are not alone in your transition from married to divorced to single life, and they will help speed up your realization about how fun your new life can be.

During this period, see your life coach and psychiatrist once a week, both of them if you can. Really be honest with yourself. Confront those very hard issues and begin to delve into what you want in your romantic life and life in general, for both the short and long term.

And don't forget to have fun! With so much in flux initially and so many new things to deal with, life can become too serious. Lighten up and internalize all the silver linings coming your way.

For the longer term, get specific about what you want and need in a partner, in **_great_** detail. Prioritize these traits, and decide which ones are deal breakers if they're not there. Also think about whether you really want a long-term relationship. Maybe, for now, you only want something shorter term.

To help you get clear on your dating/mate preferences, I've developed the following questions to ask yourself. (I've included comments on my own preferences as examples.) Once you get clear, you can also ask your dates these questions to learn their preferences:

1. Age range: What age range are you looking for? For me, age range is 35 to 50 (at the time of this writing I am 53). Rationale: Part of my self-evaluation was that I would strongly prefer not to have any more children (I already have three: a 29-year-old stepson, an 18-year-old son, and a 16-year-old daughter), but given my high-energy levels and strong libido, I needed to be with a younger woman. This age range facilitated both.

2. Physical appearance: How important is this to you? What is your range—from gorgeous to attractive to pleasant looking? We all know that men are generally more visually oriented and often put a higher premium on looks than women do. Understand this about yourself if you are a man, and know what you need and want in the looks of your partner.

    For example, I prefer petite, in-shape, and feminine women. Ideal for me is 5'1" to 5'7", 100 to 120 pounds. I am 5'10" and want to be taller than my partner, even when she's in heels, and I want to be able to pick her up and carry her.

    I have found that women tend to be more forgiving on the physical front. Even so, you need to know what you want in this category.

3. Personality: Do you want strong, outgoing, high libido, assertive, loquacious, intelligent, entrepreneurial, independent, self-reliant, financially independent or more passive, deferential, traditional? Know what you want and go after that!

I want an intelligent, independent, strong, and assertive woman, but also one who is feminine, affectionate, passionate, and extremely communicative. Having a strong libido and being mischievous, open-minded, and adventuresome are also essential.

4. Dress/attire/style: What do you like? Dresses and heels? Casual but sexy? Business attire? (Don't laugh. Many men and women find business attire very alluring!) I like the strong feminine look: dresses and heels. Though this is one of the few aspects of your partner that you can influence over time, it is still important.

5. Activity level: Do you want someone who works out in a gym or prefers outdoor exercise such as hiking and swimming? Or dancing? Though you do not need to share the same activities, a general compatibility in overall activity levels is important. And how often do they exercise and why? Many people throw their energy into working out when they have a relationship deficiency, so observe how they handle this. The whole health/working out/eating arena is an important, psychological issue and a good one to explore and examine on that first date. (See detailed discovery issues later in this chapter.)

6. Strong likes/dislikes: What do you really love/hate to do? Dining? Traveling? Sailing? Movies? Arts? Dancing? These types of activities are important to have in common with your partner. So know what you like and what you want to share with a partner. This is also a good discovery item on the first date.

For example, I determined that a love of eating was an important desire to share. So for me, nothing kills the joy of a great restaurant and dining experience than a partner who orders only a salad and then barely eats it.

7. Friends/family: How important is it to you that your partner be involved and committed to friends and family? What does that say about them to you? Do they have long-term friends? Do they have good relationships with their parents and siblings? Though not without exception, this can tell you a lot about their commitment to communication and long-term relationships in general, as well as flexibility, selfishness, give and take, etc. I believe it is an important issue to explore and also one that lends itself to first-date exploration.

8. Kids: Do you want kids or maybe more kids? Obviously, this is an important issue. Kids are a lifetime commitment, and this is a massive life-altering decision. Also of critical importance is the question of whether you want and can accept your partner's kids in your life. What ages are acceptable? Young children ages two to seven affect the relationship totally differently than teenagers do. Explore this question with yourself and your life coach and therapist.

    I know that I strongly do not want any more kids. I learned how I felt through a lovely six-month relationship with a 36-year-old woman in New York. I was 48 at the time. She really wanted children, and though I was very much in love with her, I decided, after much wrenching self-examination, that I had to let her go. For her sake, I had to end the relationship so she could have her children, because I could not go there. Very happily, she met someone a few years later, and at the age of 40, she had her first son. We are still good friends and meet regularly for coffee, with her son in tow!

9. Chemistry: What about chemistry? Of course, strong chemistry is virtually a universal requirement, but it is important to understand how you feel about it. Chemistry is one of the most enigmatic and intangible elements between two people. We all wish we could tell who we will have chemistry with, but in my experience, it's either there—or not. Don't fight this one. Don't try to convince yourself that there is or will be chemistry if there isn't. If you don't feel strong chemistry right away, you'll never feel it strong enough to sustain a long-term relationship. Chemistry is a big part of the glue that keeps a relationship together.

   At the same time, off-the-charts chemistry is also not sustainable, as eventually it will burn itself out. Overwhelming chemistry is incredibly fun while it lasts, but it keeps many of the other relationship attributes from developing properly so that, when the passion eventually and inevitably cools, the relationship falls flat.

   The only way to determine whether an initial attraction will last beyond first impressions is to spend time together. I believe this is properly discovered through the first few dates and the first holding and kissing times. If you are like most people, you will know the true nature of your chemistry only when you really kiss romantically, and you need to put in a little time to get to that optimal kissing moment. More on that later.

10. Habits: What habits can you accept—and which ones drive you crazy? Habits to seriously consider and observe in your partner include smoking, level and manner of alcohol consumption, level of neatness or messiness, drug use, snoring,

table manners and overall manners, personal hygiene, and chronic bad breath. These are the obvious and higher profile habits, but explore your own sensitivities as far as personal habits and conduct are concerned. Since they occur so frequently, if not recognized and addressed, they can be a devastating and undermining force in a relationship.

READY TO DATE

At last! Your six months of waiting, self-exploration, and self-development is over. So how do you start dating? What do you do first?

You probably still aren't fully ready for a committed relationship. (I believe, as do most life coaches and psychiatrists, that you need at least one to two years following the finalized divorce before you are ready.) Your early steps should be about getting out there, meeting people and learning to date again, rather than steps toward a deep connection. What you want to achieve is having a lot of fun, learning through practice what you want and like, and perhaps most importantly, developing your dating skills.

For now, you want to start with more long shots than real attempts to finding a lasting match. Some of the more long-shot dating sources include:

1. <u>Other people still in the divorce process or recently out of it</u>: These people pose little danger of either of you seeking something long term with each other. You can find them from friends and online (see Chapter 5).

2. <u>Online dating</u>: Whether match.com, eHarmony, or JDate. com, these excellent resources work on volume. (See Chapter 5

on the pros of online dating, matchmakers, and dating services.) Through these services, you can have virtually unlimited sources for early dating.

3. <u>Random meetings out in the world</u>: These are fun and unpredictable, but also not high likelihood sources. If you see someone attractive, approach him/her kindly and with great respect and ask him/her out. I made a commitment to myself to always do this, and it has been surprisingly productive and great fun. Most people when approached are flattered, and I would say approximately 75 percent of the time, they agree to meet for a coffee or a drink. And when they say yes, it feels great! Add this to your repertoire, especially early on when you don't care as much that the likelihood is low of meeting a great match!

In the first six months of dating, stay away from the better sources, which are friend referrals and dating and matchmaking services (see Chapter 5 for in-depth detail).

So if you are initially sourcing dates that are unlikely to lead to anything serious, what are the goals of this initial dating phase?

Simply put, the answer is fourfold. You want to start:

1. Having some fun
2. Enjoying great sex again
3. Developing your dating skills
4. Building your non-married friends network

Most married couples are friends with other married couples. So one of the initially hardest challenges after you separate is to start building a social network of single people.

Dates you go on but don't click with can still play an important role—they can be a good source of people for your singles social network. This is a critical component to rebuilding your new life. And it's fun. Once your network gets going, it can become a valuable source of meeting new dates. Friends of friends can be great dates!

What does developing your dating skills mean? Well, it means learning how to keep a lively and interesting conversation going and to *listen* well. It also means learning how to get all of those important first-date questions answered without it seeming like a grand inquisition. Remember, the main and only substantive goal of the first date, other than just having fun (which is also important), is to decide whether you want a second date!

Developing your dating skills also involves perfecting your gentlemanly skills for the men and your lady skills for the women. (I'll discuss this more later on.) You also want to learn what the great date locations are for drinks or dinner (only second dates or later), discover where to take your dates for weekend getaways or longer excursions, and develop your dating confidence and experience. Like anything else, dating is a skill, and you improve with practice. So practice, practice, practice!

KEY QUESTIONS TO GET ANSWERED ON THE FIRST DATE

Managing the dynamics of the first date is an important skill, and as just mentioned, it takes practice. Be patient with yourself, because you haven't done this in many years. You will be that much better at managing your dating life after you read this book and go out on some dates. With all the information and research contained here, you will need far fewer dates to hone your skills than I needed!

Let's start with the key first-date issues and questions that will help you decide whether you want a second date:

- Does he/she want kids?
- Does he/she have kids and how old are they?
- What is his/her custody arrangement? (Gives you an idea of his/her availability and flexibility.)
- Does he/she like to travel?
- Does he/she communicate and express well?
- Did he/she pick up on your innuendos and double entendres and how did he/she react to them?
- How traumatic was his/her divorce and what were the reasons for the divorce? In that description, is there a concession that it was not all the ex's fault? (It is never completely one sided, so a recognition of his/her part in the divorce shows perspective and humility.)
- Is he/she cordial with his/her ex? (Beware the nightmare ex scenario.)
- How long was the marriage or other serious relationship? (Gives you an idea of his/her staying power and commitment ability.) By the way, having three or more marriages in his/her history is a big red flag!
- Do you feel comfortable with his/her eye contact?
- What does she/he do professionally? (Gives you an idea of her/his schedule and availability as well as her/his need for intellectual challenge.)
- What does he/she do in his/her free time? Sports? Arts? Hiking? Reading? Music?

- Does he/she like to eat? What does he/she like to eat? Is he/she a foodie?

- Is he/she a morning or an evening person?

- What about lifestyle, vacation, days off? This is an often-overlooked question but is one of the most important. If you are a traveler and like spontaneous activities, you will be very frustrated with a partner who has a conventional 9 to 5 job with two weeks' vacation.

- What is your date's relationship to her/his father and mother and siblings? For men, their relationship with their mothers is key, and vice versa for women. This is critical. Not that a problematic parental relationship can't be overcome, but it is a major hurdle. Much better to be with someone who has a great, loving, and communicative relationship with both parents but especially with the key opposite-sex parent. Delve into this deeply. Find out what that relationship is like and was like growing up, whether the parents were supportive of his/her marriage (if there was one), and whether they liked your date's spouse, and how often he/she sees and talks to them.

  Though not quite as important as the parents, your date's relationship with siblings is worthy of a few questions. Find out how many there are and what sex and their birth order and how close they are to each other. Find out about the depth and frequency of their contact.

  Your date's relationships to parents and siblings will give you important insight into your date's ability and willingness to maintain long-term and close relationships even when they are not easy to maintain. These relationships will also give you an indication of the modeling and example that your date had while growing up—an important indicator for you to consider.

All this may seem like a lot to address on your first date, which usually lasts anywhere from 45 minutes to an hour and a half, but as you develop your skill, you will find it happens quite naturally.

WHAT TO WEAR?

What your date wears on the first outing says volumes about him/her, so pay attention! Of course you don't want to attribute too much significance to anything so shallow as clothing, but what each of you wears makes a statement, especially on the first few dates. What you each wear on the first few dates contributes to important visual impressions. What you wear can also send some messages about your personality, so give your outfits some careful consideration.

For you men, since so many men don't dress well, a well-put-together outfit says a lot—that you care about how you look and that you have a more creative and stylish side to you. On those first few dates especially, wear a nice collared shirt with stylish jeans and, depending on the time of day and location of the date, perhaps an attractive sports jacket. And don't forget your shoes. They show you pay attention to detail, and they complete your outfit with style.

For you women, as usual, it isn't quite fair, but your outfits over the first few dates will be highly scrutinized and evaluated by your date. Carefully consider how revealing you want the outfits to be. Wear heels for sure because men love them and find them sexy. Dresses or skirts are much more preferable to pants. Pay attention to how your hair is arranged. If you have long hair, wear it down, because it is much sexier and more attractive, while hair up sends a more conservative and restrained message. Err on the side of less makeup. Generally, men don't like too much makeup and want to see what you really look like. Don't overly accessorize; defer to just a few nice pieces of jewelry.

Now let's look at this from the other perspective. For you men, see whether she is wearing anything at all revealing. This offers commentary on how comfortable she is with her body and in her own skin and a hint about her sexuality. Is she wearing a dress (much more feminine) or pants, high heels (more fashionable and way more sexy), or flats (more conservative and reserved)? How much makeup is she wearing and how do you feel about it? Does she wear lipstick or lip gloss, and does she reapply it constantly? Many men don't like kissing lipstick or lip gloss, and if she is addicted to either of these, you may be kissing it a lot!

For you women, was he able to put together a decent outfit? Is it hip or stylish? This shows he cares about how he looks and took the time to make it happen. Check out his shoes. They say a lot about his sense of style and attention to detail. How open is his shirt? Does he wear a lot of jewelry, and is it too loud? Do his clothes emphasize or minimize his body? This might give you a glimpse as to how comfortable he is in his own skin, not to mention giving you a good snapshot of how nice his body is.

Underwear, once exposed, is very important. "Tighty whiteys" are a turn off to almost all women! So men, revamp your entire underwear collection, as you never know when they will see the light of day. For you women, you tend to already wear nice, sexy underwear, but take a review look and spruce it up if needed. Men generally love beautiful undergarments on women.

EYE CONTACT

Comfortable eye contact is important. For inexplicable reasons, sometimes we can be either very comfortable or very uncomfortable with someone else's eye contact. Obviously, for there to be any chance of something developing, you have to be comfortable in your date's eye contact. Seems so obvious, but many people discount this. Don't!

DECISION TIME

After the first date is over, you should be able to easily decide whether or not to go on the second date.

If you find yourself struggling with this decision, then it's a no-go. For dating practice early on, it is totally fine to go out again, but once you are through the first 6 to 12 months of dating, you don't want to waste either of your time. If the relationship has real potential, you should feel excited to go out again, right away. We all have the tendency to try to convince ourselves that we *should* go out with that person again. DON'T DO THIS. If it isn't obvious, clear cut, and powerful, it is never going to be that great a relationship.

SECOND DATE AND BEYOND

You've decided. You definitely want to see your date again. The second date and beyond should include lots of dinners, walks, hikes, outings of extended duration. You want to see how much you like being together, pay attention to how strong the chemistry is, and learn as much about the person and her/his background, family, friends, and relationship history as possible. Let it all sink in, and if you still want to be with her/him, that is the sign you are looking for. Do you start missing the person after a few days have passed? Obviously, that is a good and very important sign.

WHAT ABOUT THE WHOLE TREATING/PAYING ISSUE?

I am a bit old school on this one. I feel that the man should pay the first few times, but then the woman should treat for something, even if it is a smaller item, like the movies or ice cream. The ongoing pattern as you start seeing each other more regularly should be dictated by what each of you can afford. If you can both afford it, then over time I believe it is healthy to share the costs of what you do together. If, on the other hand, one of you has many more financial resources than the other, then I believe that you each should contribute according to your ability. So the one with less can treat for movies and ice cream, while the other takes care of the larger items. Regardless, I believe that it is important that both people contribute financially. Not only is this fair, it also shows an awareness and appreciation of what the other person is doing. As you get into the relationship, if something doesn't feel quite right regarding the payment issue, bring it up and discuss it.

I have to share a quick, strange story from my dating life. I am always more than happy to treat for the first few dates and even beyond, but in this case I soon discovered that my partner had a strange belief that the man should essentially pay for everything, always, regardless! She would want to pay only for birthday presents or other similar items. Her belief had nothing to do with her means, as she was very affluent, but she had somehow developed this strange perspective on paying. Over time, it started to really bother me, as it seemed so unnatural. (Of course, I ran it by my shrink and she totally agreed.) So I brought it up, and she was still reluctant to share expenses. Though this wasn't a deal breaker, it was undoubtedly a strange and unpleasant contributor to the deterioration of our relationship. This extreme example reemphasizes the importance of knowing and asking for what you want and talking about issues that come up to see whether you can live with that person or possibly ask them to change that behavior.

LONG DISTANCE RELATIONSHIPS

This is a very tricky issue. On the positive side, distance can keep relationships exciting and fresh. While you are apart, you miss each other and are so excited when you get together. On the negative side, however, you have to be apart sometimes for long stretches and your heart aches for your partner. But just as importantly, you miss out on sharing so many things together. My conclusion regarding long distance relationships is that they are manageable as long you have two essential items:

1. You both make a commitment to not allow more than some relatively limited amount of time to pass between visits. I suggest a maximum of two weeks and preferably no more than 7 to 10 days.

2. You have a plan to eventually end the long distance and be together. An open-ended long distance relationship is extremely difficult to sustain. It is a formula for heartache and angst, and I strongly discourage pursuing one that appears to have no

possibility of ever becoming a relationship where you can see each other more regularly and with less separation—unless, of course, that makes you happy! For most, it does not.

TIME APART

Limited time apart is very healthy for a relationship. It makes each of you more interesting and creates more things to share. Unfortunately, many couples suffer from overexposure when they are almost never apart; excessive exposure breeds contempt and frustration. Create a way to have time on your own, and make sure your partner knows it is not in the least bit personal. Plan weekends away with your buddies a few times a year. Both partners should do this. It maintains your great friendships and adds to the excitement of getting back together with your partner. Besides, it's really nice to be alone at home sometimes. Don't ignore this perfectly natural need and desire, as so many do. Too much time together can build resentment, frustration, and anger. (This falls under the commandment of not allowing anything to fester, which we'll explore in Chapter 11.)

GOING AWAY TOGETHER

I advocate going away together as early as is comfortable and setting it up so it's easy to be comfortable. What does this mean? If you are really interested and it feels right, invite your date to go away for a few days, but insist that it include separate rooms to eliminate any sexual or proximity pressure. Especially early on, it is really nice to have your own space and your own bathroom.

What does going away do for a young relationship? It creates a relaxed space for the two of you to spend extended high-quality time together that normal dating cannot possibly do. A long weekend together is the equivalent of more than a whole month's worth of conventional dating. It speeds up your ability to see whether you have real potential. The concentrated nature of being away together shows you clearly how well you get along and how strong the chemistry is between you. And when you are away together, there are many little decisions to make, and these dynamics also shed highly instructive light on your compatibility. Besides, it's great fun to go somewhere beautiful and romantic with your new love interest!

Some people argue that your ability to evaluate compatibility from an early getaway is obscured by the dazzle of the honeymoon phase. I say that the early years will be part of the honeymoon phase regardless, so why not accelerate things to see whether you are, in fact, able to get into that honeymoon phase? Life is so short. Why not expedite things to minimize wasting each other's time?

THE BEST GETAWAY LOCATIONS

There are so many exciting places to discover together. I live in California; so naturally, I have explored that part of the world more intensely. I have included some of my favorite romantic spots in the western U.S., Mexico, and beyond. Admittedly, some of them are expensive, but well worth it if you can afford them.

ROMANTIC GETAWAYS

Domestic Spots

<u>Napa or Sonoma valley wine country</u>: One of the most beautiful and romantic spots. Perfect for walks, wine tasting, picnics, and many superb restaurants. For a once-in-a-lifetime epicurean experience, book months ahead at The French Laundry. My favorite hotel in the region is Hotel Les Mars, a Relais & Chateaux property, in Healdsburg. Other favorites include Auberge du Soleil, Meritage, and Meadowood.

––––––––––

<u>Vegas</u>: You can't go wrong with Vegas as a fun and surprisingly romantic getaway. The clear hotel standouts for couples' visits are the Bellagio or the Wynn. Today's Vegas offers world-class restaurants, spas, and shopping and, of course, great people-watching scenes everywhere (but especially at the pools). For those who like it, gambling, especially with craps, is a fun activity to do together. If you are a steak lover, Delmonico's in the Venetian is an absolute-must visit.

––––––––––

<u>Health spas and resorts</u>: The clear standouts in this category are the two Canyon Ranch resorts, one in Tucson, Arizona, and the other in the Berkshires (Lenox, Massachusetts). I also like the Miraval, which is also in Tucson. The scenery is fantastic and the food extremely healthy and delicious. For those of you who are athletically inclined, this is a great getaway option. Working out together, doing yoga, hanging out in the spa, and so on, are all wonderful relationship activities.

––––––––––

<u>Disneyland/Disneyworld</u>: Admittedly these are not for everyone, but are fun places for a couple, especially during the off-season and during the week, when it is much less crowded. They feature very nice hotels, restaurants, and workout facilities and spas, so you can have a great vacation at these parks.

<u>San Francisco</u>: One of the great cities in the United States, with lots to do together. The city is spectacularly beautiful, especially when the weather is good, with a superb and innovative restaurant scene. Overall, I consider this a very romantic city. Best getaway weekend places to stay include the Ritz Carlton and the Four Seasons. Lots of lovely B&Bs, too.

<u>Laguna Beach, California</u>: One of the best beach cities between San Diego and LA, this town offers great galleries, restaurants, and beautiful beaches. My favorite place to stay is undoubtedly The Montage, an elegant resort built right over the ocean, boasting two superb restaurants, a well-equipped gym and spa, and two pools, one for families and one just for couples. Not to be missed is the spectacular great room as you first enter the hotel; it overlooks the ocean and features a talented piano player and a roaring fireplace.

The newly renovated Ritz Carlton is also spectacular and provides a comparable experience to the Montage. The beach access and experience is noteworthy and the views are unparalleled.

<u>Big Sur/Carmel, California</u>: Arguably the most beautiful spot on the West Coast, this place is a magical and breathtaking combination of dramatic vistas, spectacular hiking, fantastic spas, attractive galleries and shops, a world-famous aquarium, excellent restaurants, and awe-inspiring hotels. The best hotel by far is The Post Ranch Inn (though very expensive), which features gorgeous rooms built into the cliff, overlooking the ocean, and tree house rooms, where else, up in the trees! The hotel also offers a stunning endless pool overlooking the water, a super restaurant perched in the cliff, a great spa, and walking and hiking trails.

A distant second is the Ventana Inn, across the street, which also has a very nice restaurant.

<u>Mackinac Island, Michigan</u>: A lovely, secluded pedestrian-only island north of Chicago. A charming, unusual getaway that's best, of course, in the summer months, when you can rent bicycles and tour the island. Very quaint restaurants and an old world-style Grand Hotel.

<u>Tanglewood</u>: Tanglewood is a renowned music venue in Lenox, Massachusetts, that has been the summer home of the Boston Symphony Orchestra since 1937. Besides classical music, Tanglewood hosts the Festival of Contemporary Music and a jazz festival featuring popular artists' concerts. There are many romantic B&Bs nearby this excellent outdoor music venue.

<u>New York City</u>: Not much I can add about this city of world-class restaurants, clubs, and theaters. Best places to stay include the

St. Regis and the Ritz Carlton, along with many new boutique hotels. One of the best walking cities in the world, and, of course, Central Park is unrivaled for a city park, with endless things to do there. Not to be missed are the breathtaking and deeply moving memorial to 9/11 and the gorgeous new buildings around Ground Zero.

<u>Miami</u>: An exciting, hip spot that feels international and cosmopolitan. Best known for its pulsating night life and restaurants and, of course, fantastic beaches, Miami is also a great weekend getaway location. The best romantic hotels include the Mondrian, The Setai, Ritz Carlton, Fountainbleu, St. Regis, and the Delano.

Foreign Spots

<u>Paris</u>: The most romantic and beautiful city in the world. Admittedly, going to Paris is rather extravagant at any time, but especially early on in a relationship; however, sometimes it is just the right place to go! The George V is my unreservedly top-recommended hotel. Expensive, spectacularly elegant, and well appointed, this hotel boasts some of the best-trained staff in the world. Their lobby flower arrangements are works of art, and Le Cinq, the hotel's fine dining restaurant, consistently ranks in the top 10 restaurants in Paris. If you bond with your waiters and team (usually 8 to 10 people catering to you during your meal), you might be invited for a tour of the kitchen, which is a real treat! Not only are there more than 40 people working there, but the intricacy, skill, and deep care with which every single item is prepared is awesome.

Needless to say, Paris is perhaps the best walking city in the world, filled with awe-inspiring parks, architecture, and some of the most beautiful museums in the world. The quality of the food is world renowned, and the alleged French aloofness is so overstated. The palpable sensuality and sensuousness of the Parisian culture is unique and inspiring: the people dress elegantly, even in everyday situations, with a subtle sensual pride; the shops are beautiful and creatively stocked; and the avenues and boulevards are wide, grand, and incomparable.

Food everywhere in Paris is noteworthy, even in the street. Crepes and sandwiches on almost every block are delicious. The fine dining restaurants are unrivaled in the world.

London: This cosmopolitan city has vastly improved its culinary standing, which now complements its wonderful history and charm and its dynamic night life and theater. London attracts people from all over the world, so the feeling in the city is truly global. Claridges is my top hotel recommendation, a classic old building beautifully renovated with world-class service. Despite its completely deserved status of having the worst weather of any city in the world, it is nevertheless a great walking city! Also well worth exploring is the beautiful countryside just outside London, where you will feel like you were transported back 200 years into an idyllic and picturesque setting.

Rome: This city rivals the beauty of Paris and exceeds it in terms of awe-inspiring antiquity in full display, which is wonderfully integrated into the modern and bustling yet vibrant city. The culture, refinement, and sophistication of the Ancient Roman civilization is truly astounding the more you learn, and the Renaissance period's presence highlighted by St. Peter's and the Sistine Chapel never cease to inspire. Restaurants are spectacular, and you can never have enough pizza and gelato while you are there! I especially recommend staying at the St. Regis in Rome, as it is perfectly situated for easy walks to the highlights of the ancient city and is housed in a beautifully restored old building with dramatic common areas and beautifully appointed, classic Romanesque decor. Their daily buffet breakfast is memorable.

———————

Cabo San Lucas in Mexico: For a great beach getaway, Cabo is superb. The best place to stay for couples is Las Ventanas, an elegant resort that offers service and food that doesn't feel like Mexico. It is a small, romantic resort with no kids, so it is perfect for couples. Cabo has a beautiful beach, a lovely spa, and excellent workout facilities. The one main restaurant offers delicious food, and the daily delivery of fresh juices to your room in the morning is a delightful touch. It is a small and intimate place, where you hardly see other people. One very romantic offering is a private sunset dinner for two on the beach, which I highly recommend.

———————

Hara Mara Retreat outside of Puerta Vallarta, Mexico: A breathtakingly beautiful spot, designed as a yoga retreat, featuring gorgeous views of the ocean and a clean, wholesome and delicious cuisine with no meat.

In addition to yoga, they have massage and other treatments, open-air thatched rooms, and a lovely local town called Sayulita. You will feel a million miles away from it all.

———————

<u>Caribbean</u>: For East Coasters this is much more convenient than Mexico and perhaps more beautiful and equally romantic and also offers great cuisine. Best places include Turks and Caicos, St. Bart's, and St. Marten, as well as several very small, exclusive islands.

<u>Bermuda</u>: A beautiful old-world spot only a little over an hour's flight from the East Coast. Still a British territory, which features lovely beaches, several five-star grand hotels, and romantic restaurants.

More Cost-effective Getaways

When time or money becomes a limiting factor, you still have many wonderful ways to create the "away" dynamic. As we all know, merely a change in surroundings does wonders for us, helping us to put away the daily tasks and thoughts. So consider driving to the next town and staying in a reasonably priced hotel, or get up very early and plan a whole day of activities until late in the evening. Such a day will feel like you have been away and will provide you with much of the same insights that an actual getaway would. Consider going camping or renting an RV, both of which are considerably less expensive than a hotel.

DO WHAT YOU LOVE TO DO

I believe strongly that in doing what you love to do, you increase your chances of meeting a potential partner during the course of these activities. But, in addition to that, you can consciously put yourself in places where the odds of meeting people are greatly increased.

Great Places to Meet Women:

- Yoga classes and yoga retreats are made up of approximately 80 percent beautifully in-shape, scantily clothed women.
- Health spas and resorts are 65 percent populated by women.
- Athletic activities, like Backroads and Club Med, which are interactive and social, attract many singles and provide a relaxed way to meet a whole group of people.
- Grocery stores are surprisingly productive! You can easily engage someone with a question about some product you are looking for.
- Gyms are a naturally interactive environment with a lot of single people.
- Horseback riding events are a sport heavily dominated by women and have a lot of downtime for interactions.
- Personal growth seminars and conferences put on by organizations such as Tony Robbins and Landmark Education usually have a significant majority of women.
- Charity events attract a lot of single people, and they encourage good conversations and interest-sharing opportunities with your potential partner.

Great Places to Meet Men:

- Sports bars are 80 percent populated by men.
- Sports events are attended by over 70 percent men.
- Conferences, especially financial ones, attract over 80 percent male attendees.

- Men's fine clothing stores, where you will find upscale elegant men who care about how they look!
- Sailing, a very social sport, includes a high percentage of men.
- Gyms are a natural place to meet both men and women.
- Charity events are a great place for meeting men and women.

TEXTING/EMAILING PROTOCOL

In today's multimedia and social media world, texting and emailing will and should be part of your dating and relationship life. They can be a wonderful supplement to your phone and in-person interactions. The key word in the previous statement is "supplement."

Be very careful not to allow texting to dominate your interactions. Because texting is so easy and so much a part of our day-to-day lives, it's easy to overdo. It is absolutely essential that you never discuss anything of any real substance through texting. Not only can texting easily cause miscommunication, but also several layers of important interaction—such as eye contact, body language, and tone of voice—are obviously nonexistent in texting. With any topic of substance and importance, you need to communicate face-to-face or at least on the phone. I have learned about the risks and dangers of texting the hard way. I have had several very tricky situations evolve (see Chapter 10) out of texting miscommunications.

BEWARE THE ENSNARER

There are quite a few single people out there who are looking to ensnare a long-term partner through marriage by essentially tricking them. Their approach is to be the person with attributes you want them to have—but these attributes are not their true characteristics. Some of these people are really good at it. At the risk of generalizing, more of them are women than men, as what drive many of them is their fear of being alone and their fear of financial insecurity. Men tend to have these fears less frequently.

Besides just being observant and a good judge of character, the best way to flush out the truth about an ensnarer is twofold:

First, don't make any commitments too quickly. Anyone who is quickly pushing commitment, living together, etc., has some kind of unhealthy agenda. With important topics like that, rushing is never a good idea. Waiting never has a downside in these situations. Suggesting that you both give a relationship some time puts pressure on the ensnarer. He/she doesn't want to have to maintain these false characteristics for too long.

Second, talk about how you want to enjoy this stage and each stage in your relationship for a long time. This should be true anyway, but if you suspect any possible ensnaring, this has a good chance of flushing it out. Again, the prospect of an extended time period for maintaining the ensnaring strategy is very unappealing to the ensnarer.

Also, as the relationship gets more serious, discuss the issues of long-term commitment, living together, and marriage, as you should in any relationship. In the case of the suspected ensnarer, watch very carefully how your partner reacts. The ensnarer will be extremely serious and intense with regard to these topics. He/she will, of course, try to hide this intensity, but the signs are usually there if you watch for them.

HAVE A CHAT/DISCUSSING SEX

Sometime over the first few dates, see whether you can bring up an open and frank chat about sex. Not only will your partner's manner and body language tell you a lot about how comfortable she/he is about sex, but you will also learn a lot about her/his preferences, likes, fantasies, etc. Plus it's a fun topic to talk about and one that we don't talk about enough. Too often we treat it as taboo, but it shouldn't be. Also, this is one of those chats that will bring you much closer to each other (as is so often true with more vulnerable and disclosure-oriented discussions).

So in this chat, ask about desired frequency, favorite positions and why, orgasm and what type of stimulation optimizes orgasm, and clitoral versus vaginal orgasm and her G spot. Talk about how much you both like oral sex and what particularly feels good, fantasies, each of your feelings about being tied up and dressing up, sex in public places, as well as things you might not like. Discuss your feelings about anal sex, condoms, testing for STDs, and anything that is on your mind. This chat is not a substitute for the very directed discussion I so strongly recommend that all couples have before they are going to have sex (see Chapter 6), which is specifically focused on developing an agreed upon approach to birth control, abortion, and STD prevention.

In one of my recent relationships, I had this sex chat on a plane after only three dates, and it lasted almost two hours! She had never in her life had a chat like it. She told me she was fascinated by it—and quite titillated. All great signs, by the way. I was surprised by how she embraced this discussion, and despite her more reserved demeanor, how sexual she was, which was strongly reaffirmed once we started having sex.

TELLING THE KIDS ABOUT YOUR DATING LIFE

This tricky issue requires a great deal of sensitivity and judgment. You need to know your kids and what they are ready and able to know. (It's worth discussing with your life coach and therapist first.) The goal is to be as honest and open with them as their age, development, and mentality will permit. Generally, kids want their parents to be happy and to have a partner, and if their mother and father can't live together, they want both of them to find someone else to be happy with.

But if the divorce has created too much uncertainty and instability for the kids, they might not be ready to hear about your dating life. That is why you need to gradually feel them out, especially as more time goes by and the initial shock of the divorce wears off, and they become accustomed to the new reality.

MALE/FEMALE PHYSICALITY

I am often asked why men and women are physically evaluated so differently by society. Why is it that a 50-year-old man with gray hair is deemed distinguished and good looking with "salt and pepper hair," while a 50-year-old woman with the same color of hair is often looked at less positively? Here's my take after much research:

Over the millennia, men were the providers of food and shelter, and women were the child bearers. Concurrently, men had multiple partners to optimize survival rates, so women competed more for men and did so by being physically attractive. As a result, men evolved to be more visual, women less so. This has led to a society that celebrates women's physicality: her legs, especially in heels; cleavage;

and her body in general, which is displayed all over the media. This phenomenon is much less true for men because women evolved to value physical and financial security more so than physical attributes. Financially successful women are generally less appealing to men than are financially successful men to women.

I mention this physicality issue because I am asked about it frequently, especially by my women clients. I want to encourage all of us to just accept it whether we like it or not. It has been formed over thousands of years, and it is not going to change any time soon.

PROPER BREAKING-UP PROTOCOLS

Sometimes, for all the warnings and advice, the relationship just doesn't work. If you're a decent human being, breaking up is unpleasant, and it's even worse to be broken up with! I find most people find it difficult to break up properly, which makes it excruciating to all involved.

However, despite the intrinsic challenges of almost all breakups, there are some important protocols that need to be followed and adhered to. A breakup should always be done in a manner that reflects and respects the duration and the nature of the relationship. Here are my specific recommendations regarding the manner of a breakup:

- After only one date: No breakup required. You both can just disappear.

- After two to three dates: A simple phone call is the right thing to do to tell the other person that you appreciated the time together but that it just isn't quite working for you. The two- to three-date relationship is a gray area, as you can just disappear here too, but it is kinder to call and save the other person wondering what happened to you.

- After four or more dates, I believe the right thing to do is to break up in person, face-to-face. I know it is unpleasant, but given the time and experiences that you have shared, you owe it to each other to be direct, honest, and in person.

While I do strongly advocate an honest breakup, that is, that you should tell your partner why you are ending the relationship, I also want you to consider the following: If the main reason is something that your partner can never do anything about, then soften your remarks. There is absolutely no reason to make him/her feel worse than necessary, especially if he/she can't learn or change from your input. Be honest but also considerate.

***

Embrace as many of these dating suggestions and recommendations as you feel comfortable doing, and you will not only have much more fun in your dating endeavors, but you will also be much more productive and efficient with your time. And remember that the key to successful dating is to have a positive attitude, put yourself out there, have fun, and always know that it is a numbers game. The more people you meet, the greater the likelihood you'll meet someone special.

CHAPTER 2

■

WHAT 300 SINGLES SAY ABOUT DATING, SEX, AND RELATIONSHIPS

IN ADDITION TO MY PROFESSIONAL WORK WITH COUPLES AND MY personal experience as a single man for the past eight years, I interviewed more than 300 single people about their dating experiences and relationships. In this chapter, I share with you the highlights of my research, including the top preferences and complaints from both men and women. Of course, nothing in relationships is absolute or certain, and all of us can only do the best we can. Read this chapter and learn what you can from these opinions. As you go on dates and explore this new life of yours, laugh a lot, always be honest, do your best, and enjoy the ride every minute along the way. If you conduct yourself this way, you will be more likely to have a good life with at least one great partner.

Here are some observations from the singles I interviewed:

1. Women say men wine and dine them in the early going, and then the flowers, cards, candy, and treats disappear. Men, don't stop the little gifts and gestures, ever. Men report that women are much better at maintaining the stream of nice gestures.

2. Men say women expect them to pay for too much and would like more of a balance if they can afford it.

3. Men say that they initiate the dates and activities too much. They would love for women to suggest get-togethers and activities more.

4. If he isn't calling and isn't initiating activities, he isn't that into you.

5. Women say men stop dressing nicely and grooming themselves after a while. Men, keep up your appearance. Take care of how you look.

6. Men don't like too much makeup and constant reapplication of lipstick or gloss (especially in the midst of kissing, believe it or not!).

7. Men like women to look good and dress well.

8. Men love heels.

9. Most men don't like overweight women.

10. Most women are willing to look beyond men's physical limitations, such as being overweight or bald.

11. Men think about sex all the time.

12. Women think about romance all the time.

13. Great sex is more important to men than to women.

14. Men love it when women initiate sex.

15. Men try the first kiss too early, too often.

16. Women say men are much too aggressive with their tongues on the first kiss, so, men, go easy early on.

17. Men advance sexually too early in a relationship.

18. Most women want men to be the sexual initiators and more dominant partners.

19. Most women like to be sexually dominated.

20. Women like to be picked up for dates.

21. Women prefer the missionary position.

22. Men prefer the missionary position.

23. Men value good oral sex much more than women do.

24. Men love receiving oral sex. A lot. Any time.

25. Men like giving oral sex much more than women think they do.

26. Many women have a hard time relaxing while receiving oral sex.

27. Men feel they aren't doing their jobs if women don't have orgasms.

28. The G spot is not a myth.

29. Penis girth is just as important to most women as is appropriate length.

30. Women say that a penis that is too large is often worse than one that is too small.

31. Women love their sex toys.

32. Men love women's sex toys.

33. Women like to cuddle after sex but not as much as men think they do.

34. Most men love middle-of-the-night sex.

35. Most men love morning sex.

36. Most men love nighttime sex.

37. Most men just love sex.

38. Men like quickies much more than women do.

39. Women say too many men are selfish lovers.

40. Women love it when men are gentlemen.

41. Women love romance.

42. Most women want to get a ring.

43. Most women want to be married.

44. Women share intimate sexual details with their girlfriends much more than men do with their buddies.

45. Men love to watch sports.

46. Most women are reluctant sports watchers.

47. Men say too many women get clingy and don't give them enough space.

48. Men love weekends with their buddies.

49. Men hate it when their significant others don't support their buddy weekends away.

50. Men would like their partners to go away with their girlfriends more often than they do.

51. Men love Vegas.

52. Women love Vegas.

53. Women love to shop.

54. Men hate to shop.

55. Men like spas more than women think they do.

56. Women love spas.

57. Men put on weight around their waists and women on their hips, legs, and butts.

58. Men should never answer the question, "Do I look fat in this?" with a yes.

59. Men, know your partners' cycles and make allowances during that time of the month.

60. Men love it when women cook for them.

61. Men love getting cards from women.

62. Men are much sappier than women think they are. They just hide it.

63. Women like having their own bathrooms.

64. Most men snore.

65. It's not nice to fart in bed.

66. Women like to talk on the phone.

67. Men don't like to talk on the phone.

68. Women don't like too much texting.

69. Men like to text.

70. Men love it when women text them after a date to thank them and give them some indication of how much fun they had.

71. Women love it when men are communicative and open.

72. If women want men to do something, the soft, loving approach always works. And the chances are even higher if you have had sex that day!

***

This chapter is intended to be instructive, but also entertaining. As mentioned earlier, all comments are based on actual interviews with real, contemporary single men and women, but you need to decide which ideas work for you. Hopefully, this chapter will continue to make you think about how you are in a relationship, how considerate and present you are, and how you can improve.

CHAPTER 3

■

THE TOP FOUR WAYS TO MEET PEOPLE

So now it's time to meet people. I've devised a method that delivers optimal results—but to achieve that, you need to use all four of the ways I describe below. I do understand that you might not have the time and energy to employ all four, so if that is the case, select the ones that you are most comfortable with. The more energy, enthusiasm, and confidence you have and project, the more successful each of them will be.

1. Introductions from Friends and Family

   This is a good source in terms of quality control and filtering out the best candidates because you know where they come from or you know their family and friends. So encourage your friends and family to introduce you to their single friends. Everyone knows a few single people, so ask. If you don't ask, they probably won't make the effort, and you have to keep reminding them to make intros!

But this source has a double edge. Since these intros are coming from friends and family, you have to be extremely careful not to upset your date, as it will come back to your introducer and potentially cause an awkward situation. Hopefully, you are always courteous and polite, but handle these intros with extreme care—and keep asking everyone you know to introduce you. If you keep asking, they will deliver!

2. Online Dating Sites

   The detail for these sites is covered in Chapter 5, but here I would like to address the concept. The benefit of this resource is the virtually unlimited supply of potential candidates and the cost is reasonable. The downside is the screening is nonexistent; you have to do it all yourself. And even then, you really don't know anything about these people, so the risks are higher. You can browse and look at literally hundreds of potential dates, with their detailed profiles. Though many people's pictures are old, the overall profile gives you a good idea of the person, especially after you've read a few hundred of them.

   Which brings up the issue of writing your profile. Do not take this lightly. Remember that for online dating, your profile is the first impression of you. Put some real thought into what you want to write about yourself. Basically, you don't want to be too verbose, but you want to get across the things that are most important to you in a partner. I am available by email, greatlifeafterdivorce@yahoo.com, and my website (**www.2ndchanceatromance.com**) for counseling on writing the best possible profile, so feel free to reach out.

   You need to carefully select your picture. But don't choose pictures that look better than you really look, or old ones!

3. Dating and Matchmaking Services

   This more expensive option has much higher screening characteristics than the online sites, and you have a team working on your behalf searching for matches and digesting your feedback. They get to know you and what you are looking for and give you detailed profiles of potential matches for you to evaluate. It is an excellent complement to the online dating sites. The staff is available for direct personal interaction and discussion before and after each date, and generally my experience has been that they offer a very high caliber of candidates. In Chapter 5, I go into great detail about which ones you should consider.

4. Random Out-in-the-World Meetings

   Though discounted by many, this is a very viable way of meeting dates! Make a commitment to yourself that no matter where you are, if you see someone attractive to you, you will approach and ask him/her out. Make the commitment. Make it for yourself. You will be very pleasantly surprised at how well your efforts are received. I have met dates in line at The Soup Plantation; at restaurants with the staff; in the security line at the airport; on planes, both passengers and flight attendants; in yoga class; at movie theaters; at sporting events; at hotels on vacation; or at conferences, etc. Almost any venue presents dating opportunities.

   My experience with this approach has been very encouraging. Since few people actually do this, it is most often received positively, as a flattering gesture. You need to do it kindly and with respect, and if so delivered, I have found that more than

75 percent of the time the person will agree to meet for coffee or a drink. Some locations have even better percentages, especially if you have the opportunity to engage in conversation before asking. For example, I've had success at receptions, weddings, Bar and Bat Mitzvahs, fund-raisers, classes, running races, skiing, volleyball, etc. You need to be out there to meet people, so do activities you like and be open to this approach. The opportunities are out there. It can be anywhere if you are just open and have a positive attitude.

CHAPTER 4

LIFE COACHES AND SHRINKS: ESSENTIAL PARTNERS

THIS CHAPTER ADDRESSES USING PROFESSIONALS TO FACILITATE your personal growth and learning before, during, and after a breakup or divorce. I am *hugely* in favor of using <u>both</u> a life coach and a psychologist or psychiatrist for an extended period leading up to the divorce, during the divorce process, and at least during the initial year or two of the dating and relationship period.

A divorce is one of the most brutal and uprooting experiences anyone can have, even under the best of circumstances. It is that much worse if it is hostile and adversarial, as it unfortunately often is. Most people are in an emotional vortex during this time and, even with professional assistance, will make many bad decisions and judgments. Friends and family are essential supports, and you should talk to them extensively and welcome their support. But they are rarely enough. They are biased toward you and do not have professional training.

Make the time and commit to making the best use of these professionals. You may have to go through a few before finding your perfect professional support team, but it is so worth it. After all, you would use a trainer to help you work out, so why wouldn't you get help with something so difficult and challenging as your mental health during a time of extreme adversity?

It is always beneficial to have the help of a professional when going through a major breakup or divorce. <u>Always</u>.

So, with that in mind, how do you find the right professional team for you?

Keep in mind that, like most professions, many of the people in the mental health field are not great. You need great. So ask around. Many people use professionals now, and you will receive numerous recommendations from your friends, colleagues, and family. Ask them a lot of questions and pay the most attention to those who rave about their person.

As examples of quality professionals, I will describe a specific life coach and psychiatrists/psychologists that I have encountered over the years who I believe to be true superstars in their profession. They are worth the effort and extra cost of their fee and travel time or working with them through teleconferencing or on the phone. If you would like to evaluate them for your use, please contact me through my website, www.2ndchanceatromance.com, or through my email, **greatlifeafterdivorce@yahoo.com**, and I will make the introduction. All of them are officially closed to new patients, as they are in such demand, but with my referral and introduction they will take new clients.

RECOMMENDED LIFE COACH

Michelle Saul

Michelle is based in San Diego and is the single most insightful and talented life coach I have ever encountered. She has an extraordinary ability to get to know and to understand someone quickly and incisively. She formulates specific action items quickly and guides her clients through the process with great skill, caring, and support. She is an example of a truly dedicated and profoundly talented person who will help you change your life dramatically for the better.

RECOMMENDED PSYCHIATRIST

Dr. Martha Koo

Dr. Koo is based in Los Angeles and is the most talented psychiatrist I have ever met in more than 25 years of being in therapy and having interviewed or worked with many, many professionals. She is extraordinarily intelligent and insightful and has a kind, soft, and deeply supportive manner. Her ability to quickly understand her patients and grasp the intricacies of their situations is astounding. She is extremely dedicated to her patients and her practice.

RECOMMENDED PSYCHOLOGIST

Dr. Richard Levak

Dr. Levak is based in San Diego and is one of the preeminent professionals in his field. He is extremely intelligent, empathetic, and understanding and has a wonderfully supportive, kind, and easygoing bedside manner.

Interview several potential professionals until you have that strong connection with someone. The process is similar to dating. The chemistry has to be there. All of the people recommended to you will be qualified and intelligent, but you need that connection and chemistry. After all, you will be baring your soul and discussing your deepest feelings, thoughts, fears, experiences, etc., so you must feel comfortable with this person and trust him/her. If after two or three sessions you don't feel a good connection or chemistry, move on to the next candidate.

The selection of the right life coach and the right psychologist or psychiatrist is an absolutely critical component to your learning and development and getting you into the dating world in a healthy and productive manner.

Which brings us to the decision between a psychologist and a psychiatrist. Unless you think that you might need medication for anxiety, stress, depression, or some other problem, the more important issue is finding the right fit. However, if medication is even a possibility, then you must choose a psychiatrist since psychologists cannot prescribe. You don't want to be working with a psychologist only to discover that you need medication and then have to find a psychiatrist and start the whole process of educating him/her all over again to get your prescriptions.

FIND A GOOD COUPLES COUNSELOR

As recommended in the Prologue, finding an excellent couples counselor is essential for all relationships.

I have known and worked with many couples counselors over the years, both for myself and with the many couples I have advised and counseled. It is an extremely difficult role. Think about it for a moment. In most conventional situations, the couple is coming to the couples counselor because they have major problems in their relationship, often accompanied by deep-seated anger, resentment, and/or frustration. So the counselor has to try to create a safe and open space within the context of the huge problems between the couple in the room. Not an easy task.

So how do you know whether the couples counselor is a good fit and right for the two of you?

First of all, both of you must feel comfortable in the presence of your counselor. You probably won't feel comfortable with the content all the time, but you must both feel comfortable with the person. And it must be **both** of you because without total buy in by both partners, this process, which is very difficult even under the best of circumstances, has no chance of succeeding.

Next, in those first few sessions, observe carefully how the counselor runs the session. Are you impressed with the person's intellect, style, and approach? Does there seem to be a rational chronology to the session, and is the counselor checking in with both of you and asking you for feedback? When the counselor asks a question, does he/she appear to be really listening and interested? Is the counselor acting fairly to both of you and not favoring one over the other? And most of all, do you feel a healthy connection and chemistry with the therapist? Does it feel right? It needs to, as you will be spending a lot of time and money with this person, and it should feel just like a great first date.

For example, I recommend Dr. Lily Shariat, who practices in the Los Angeles area and is a great couples counselor.

Dr. Shariat is truly gifted. She has the ability to size up the individuals in the room extraordinarily quickly and accurately grasp the nature of the dynamic between the couple. Given the stakes involved, I strongly recommend that you seriously consider using someone like Dr. Shariat. Of course, there are many other spectacular couples counselors around the country, and it may take some trial and error to find yours. But if you follow the criteria above you have a good chance of finding the right one for you.

CHAPTER 5

DATING SERVICES, MATCHMAKERS, AND ONLINE DATING SITES: THE BEST ONES AND WHICH TO AVOID AND WHY

I AM ABOUT TO SHARE INSIGHTS THAT WILL SAVE YOU HUNDREDS OF hours of time and thousands of dollars of wasted money. This chapter contains my conclusions based on years of research and experimentation as to which dating and matchmaking services are the best and which are the ones to avoid. You have tons of choices out there—tens if not hundreds of online sites among them—and I can help you navigate them.

In addition to providing you with the pros and cons of some of these choices, I discuss the optimal duration of the relationship with them, the true cost you can negotiate, and how to manage each relationship. This is a key chapter in this book—and one of the most practical. In addition, you can go to my website, **www.2ndchanceatromance. com**, for real-time updates on matchmakers and dating services, as it is obviously a very fluid topic. And feel free to email me if you have any specific question: **greatlifeafterdivorce@yahoo.com**.

ONLINE DATING SITES

Online dating sites add a meaningful contribution to a comprehensive dating approach, but they need to be properly managed. That requires you to make a certain time commitment.

Online sites have become totally mainstream and, as such, have shed not only any stigma but also have attracted millions of subscribers, among which are some fantastic matches for you. The trick is how to find them efficiently.

Interestingly, it is a vastly different experience and challenge for men compared to women in the online dating world. When women post their profiles online, they are deluged immediately with hundreds of solicitations. Part of the reason for this is that many men just look at the pictures, and if they like them, they send an email. OK, this is a strategy, though not a good one. As a result, women need to do their own searches because searching through the hundreds of emails they receive is not practical nor has that group been screened in any way for their preferences.

Both men and women need to make a specific search with the criteria that are important to them. Most of the sites, except for eHarmony, provide for subscriber searches. That way, both men and women can generate a manageable list of candidates that possess their primary criteria. Then from that list, they can send emails expressing interest. This is the way to manage the online sites and not waste time.

The top online sites are match.com, eHarmony.com, and JDate. com. There are many others for specific interests or focuses, whether religion-based (Christian Mingle); sugar-daddy arrangements (SeekingArrangement.com); or financial status (MillionaireMatch.com), for those who are more money oriented. I suggest that you limit your participation to one or two of the top sites unless you do have some specific interest or focus, and trust me, you'll find a site that focuses on that.

Sometimes these sites are just fun! Enjoy yourself! Surf and explore and see what kind of people are out there. Vary location, distance, age, race, height, etc. Mix up your criteria and just browse away.

Go to my website for helpful tips on setting up your online profile: http://2ndchanceatromance.com/

Match.com

The biggest and most popular site by far. Easy to navigate and search and constantly being upgraded. Given its size, narrowing your focus is critical. They send you daily matches, which is a good reminder to get on the site, and you can see who viewed you, who "favorited" you, who emailed you, etc. You can review whom you viewed and emailed, as well.

eHarmony

This site has a different structure than the other online sites. In order to become a subscriber, you must fill out a rather extensive questionnaire. This has the positive effect of weeding out the looky-loos and less serious participants. In addition, eHarmony has established a process of interaction whereby you and your potential match go through several rounds of questions before you are both asked if you want to contact each other directly. You always have the option of dispensing with the back-and-forth and can go direct if both people OK it. Despite its sometimes clumsy feel, the process is a good one, and I strongly recommend this site if you are serious about meeting someone and, as I advise, plan to include an online site as part of your dating strategy. This site also sends daily matches that remind you to visit the site, and you can navigate easily around your previous interactions.

JDate.com

Ostensibly this is a Jewish site, but many of the participants are not Jewish, making it a viable mainstream online resource. It is easy to navigate and has regular updates and improvements. JDate is similar in format and feel to match.com, though it has significantly fewer subscribers. As before, the best way to find good candidates is to do your own search. It also has recommended matches and other alerts to remind you to visit the site.

Tinder

A new entrant to the field but one that is quick and fun. Basically, you flip through pictures and indicate yes or no. If they are interested too, then a dialogue can begin. It is refreshingly easy and fun and has become popular.

Hinge

Another new fun site like Tinder, which matches you with friends of your friends in your Facebook friends list.

How About We

As the name suggests, howaboutwe.com provides an array of recommendations for couple's extracurricular activities, (i.e. tips for spicing up dates, books to read, events & places to check out, etc.), on top of offering the standard profile services associated with online dating. A great tool for lovebirds or singles to take advantage of!

Coffee Meets Bagel

Started by three sisters, coffeemeetsbagel.com is a family-owned business operated by the siblings and inspired by the concept of making dating as enjoyable, and accessible, as your morning coffee. They have a simple, down to earth approach to their services.

DATING SERVICES

Offline dating services can provide even more value than online dating sites. For a considerably higher fee than online dating sites, you receive personal attention and service. They spend time getting to know you and what you want. This circles back to the personal growth and discovery essentials we discussed previously because you have to know this for them to be helpful!

How It Works

Once the dating service knows what you want in a partner, they start proposing matches for you. They usually show pictures and a brief background summary, which details the proposed match's likes, dislikes, activities, education, kids, relationship history, etc. I have included a sample profile below (and have changed the name to protect the innocent!). You then review the profile and decide whether you want to go out with that person. If so, the service gives you that person's contact information, and you call to set up a date. After the date, you give the service as much detailed feedback as possible to help guide them with future introductions for you.

It is absolutely critical to your relationship with the dating services that you not only give them highly detailed feedback but that you also stay in regular contact. You need to check in with them regularly and ask how their search for you is progressing, who they are working on for you, and so on. The squeaky-wheel concept is very much applicable here.

The following is a sample of the type of bio/profile you will receive from dating services. (Note: I have redacted personal information and photos that are usually included in the profile given to you as a client.)

***

In-Person Analysis

We found Susan to look much prettier than her photos. She has an athletic, slender figure with a natural chest. Susan has a perfect complexion and a straight, white smile. When we met her, she had just come from a yoga class and was wearing no makeup. Susan was absolutely gorgeous, even without makeup. She has a preppy and sophisticated style, which was a combination of cute and sexy. Susan is lovely and very charming. She is fun and very personable, is easy to talk to and outgoing. She is also a great conversationalist, educated, and very well spoken.

About Susan

Susan is 39 years old, 5'4" with brown hair and brown eyes. She was born in Turkey and raised in New Jersey. Susan has lived in Los Angeles, California, for the past 15 years. Her parents have been happily married now for more than 40 years. They live in Los Angeles, and she is very close with them. Susan is the youngest child and has an older brother, who lives in San Francisco. She is very close to him and sees him twice a year. Susan was raised Jewish but is now more spiritual than religious. Politically, she identifies as a Democrat, but she respects other people's opinions.

Susan attended NY University, where she achieved her undergraduate in Business Law. She is currently working as an office manager for a retailing company. She works on contracts between vendors and manufacturers. She loves her job and works a normal business schedule with no travel. Previously, Susan worked as an office manager for a renewable energy company.

In her spare time, Susan enjoys tennis, dining out, listening to music, and dancing. She likes wine tastings, watching movies, and going to museums. She enjoys going to the theater and biking. She stays fit and active by kick-boxing, running, skiing, and doing Pilates five days per week. She is very well traveled and has been all over the world. Some of Susan's favorite places have been South Africa, Spain, Greece, and France. She is fluent in Turkish and French. She is a nonsmoker and a social drinker.

Susan is divorced and does not have children of her own. Her marriage lasted five years and ended due to her ex-husband's addiction issues and lack of true intimacy. Susan is looking forward to a committed relationship leading toward marriage. She is looking for someone who is honest, smart, classy, and a true gentleman.

What She Says About Herself and What She Is Looking For

"I'm honest and like to be myself. I have a kind heart, am caring, loyal, sophisticated, physically fit, and well traveled. I enjoy trying new things and challenging myself. Family and friends are near and dear to me. I have a good sense of humor, like to laugh often, and smile a lot. Am mature and playful at the same time and can be profound or silly without getting the two mixed up. I'm seeking a partner who values honesty, trust, and integrity as much as I do. He is very intelligent, well read, and culturally well rounded. I see myself with someone who is fun loving, successful, generous, dependable, reliable, and trustworthy.

***

Now you have a good feel for the level of detail and specificity that you can expect to receive from the high-end dating services. Clearly, it gives the recipient a good idea of the upcoming potential date and, very importantly, enough information to veto someone who does not seem appealing.

The top dating services, in order of preference, currently are:

- Selective Search
- Kelleher
- Elite
- Table for Six

Less desirable dating services—proceed with caution:

- Valenti International
- It's Just Lunch
- Cupid's Coach

THE TOP DATING SERVICES

Selective Search

Of all of the services I have experienced over the years, Selective is the most professional and upfront. Based in Chicago, they also have a major presence on the East and West Coasts. They are responsive and interactive and deliver exactly what they say they will deliver, which is a rarity in the dating business. What they deliver is a regular stream of exactly what you are looking for, except for chemistry as no one can anticipate or predict that. But everything else, they deliver. They are not cheap, but as with all of these services, you can and should negotiate. Contact me for specific numbers, but both the duration and total amount can be negotiated.

They are also very capable of conducting multi-city searches for those of you who are bicoastal or live in more than one city. In my case, being both bicoastal and multi-city oriented (Los Angeles, San Diego, and San Francisco), they were able to make introductions in all of those locations when I was there. They are truly interested in the feedback from each date and listen and adjust. As you will see below, not only is this rare, but it is essential to their refining their search parameters to optimize their selected candidates.

Kelleher International

Also a very professional and responsive organization. They are based in San Francisco but are able to deliver introductions throughout California and New York. When you speak to them, be sure to ask about their presence in your locations. As with Selective, negotiation of the price and duration is part of the process, so make sure you do that! They are open to a back-end success fee, and I strongly recommend you take advantage of this fee structure.

So what do you define as a success? For me, a successful introduction that deserved a success-fee bonus was one that resulted in an exclusive relationship that lasted for more than a year. Think about what your definition of success would be, and then negotiate that into your deal. It sets the right incentive for them, gives them material upside, and gives you the likelihood of the best introductions.

Elite

Elite is more focused on Southern California so probably not the best choice outside of Southern California. They provided me with a lot of introductions and were very responsive. Less expensive than Selective or Kelleher but professional and solid.

Table for Six

This service has come up with a fun and creative idea to introduce three men and three women to each other by way of sharing a dinner together at a restaurant. The experience is delightful. Given the numbers involved, your worst-case scenario is that you end up having a really fun evening, even if you are not interested in any of the three introductions. At every dinner that I attended, the men and women were all intelligent, decently dressed, fun, and engaging. I have even made some male friends from these dinners. They are only in selected cities, so check to see whether they are in yours. They currently have a presence in the San Francisco Bay Area, Orange County, and Los Angeles. Additionally, they are very reasonably priced. Well worth a look.

PROCEED WITH CAUTION

Though I hesitated, at first, to mention these, in the end I am profoundly committed to helping my readers avoid mistakes, wasted time and money, and unpleasant experiences, so I feel compelled to share my experiences and observations with everything. I readily concede that perhaps my negative experiences with the following companies might have been just a fluke, though I strongly suspect not. Companies can also change and evolve. I submit my observations for your consideration with these caveats, but also with the suggestion that if you do choose to use these, proceed with caution.

Valenti International

Founded by a very capable entrepreneur, this company at times was spectacular for me and at others less so. I had several introductions who told me that they had not met anyone for an extended time. The introductions I had were inconsistent. Some were brilliant and very appropriate, but too many were clearly not a match. I think this company can be a great source of introductions if you can get them to focus on you and your specific interests.

It's Just Lunch

This is such a good idea—to set up more casual lunches or drinks as your first date—but they just did not deliver for me, and I tried them several times. The relatively low fee, combined with their need to do high-volume business, seemed to have reduced the amount of matchmaking research they conducted for me. So I found myself matched with obviously the wrong people despite my emphatic and strongly worded feedback.

Cupid's Coach

Despite the founders' high-intelligence level, I felt they needed to add infrastructure and more reach to deliver the great matches they want to offer. I do believe they can improve and become a good source over time.

MATCHMAKERS

First, let me describe the difference between dating services and matchmakers. Both can be good, and having both, if you can afford it, provides a more diversified and varied pool of dating candidates. The dating services, though personalized, are less personal than the matchmakers. The matchmakers are the modern version of the "yenta," or the local elderly woman in the town who sets up the young people. The great matchmakers of today develop a personal relationship with each of their clients and then scour the globe for good matches. The really good ones tend to be more expensive than the dating services. So if the range for the dating services is $5,000 to $10,000 for one to two years, the best matchmakers are $10,000 to $50,000 for the same amount of time across multiple cities. You can negotiate more with the matchmakers than you can with the dating services, and you can work out a success fee, thereby reducing the upfront fee.

So who are the best matchmakers?

Janis Spindel

A true New York City character of large proportions! Janis is all in, all the time. Though based in NYC, her business is truly global in scope. She is a caricature of the modern matchmaker, seizing every opportunity to meet a potential client or match. She is in your face and direct, but she is very good. I find her authentic, honest, extremely talented, and devoted to her profession. She has built an extraordinarily large database of people, and it is growing constantly. She has an amazing memory and seemingly unending energy. Janis is also crazy busy, so if you are a client, you need to be a squeaky wheel to get maximum attention. Besides normal introductions, Janis organizes various social events of varying sizes, from smaller dinner parties to larger mixers for her clients; these are also great opportunities to meet people. She is more expensive than most, as you would expect, but you can also negotiate with her (even though she says she doesn't!). But Janis is worth it. I have met wonderful people through her, enjoyed a fulfilling one-year relationship with one of her introductions, and have made several great friends through the introductions as well.

Elle France, Dating Agent

Elle is Los Angeles-based and is cool, hip, dedicated to her clients, edgy, and very attractive. She has that uncanny ability to meet a lot of cool women and gain their trust and confidence quickly. I have enjoyed working with her immensely and recommend her unequivocally. She is willing to customize the structure of a relationship with a client and provide regular and detailed updates. She is an excellent communicator and "gets it." Elle is also great fun to be around, which really enhances the experience of working with her.

Millionaire Matchmaker Patti Stanger

Patti Stanger is New York City based, but because of the TV show, Millionaire Matchmaker, she has national reach. A very confident matchmaker, she is fiercely dedicated and ambitious, with intelligence to match. Patti has strong opinions and is stubborn, but she will give you her all. Make sure you negotiate, but rest assures that she will deliver.

CUSTOMIZED ALTERNATIVES

For those of you who don't live on either of the coasts, finding a good dating service or matchmaker is harder. Please don't despair! There is a good solution, though it can run a bit more expensive. Most of the dating services and matchmakers will offer a customized special search for you. If you are willing to travel to meet your dates, that will increase the number of potential matches for you, but even if you are not, they will find matches willing to come to you. Especially with the best of these service providers, you will find this is a very effective way to dramatically augment your dating pool.

STRATEGY AND APPROACH WITH MATCHMAKERS AND DATING SERVICES

Your basic strategy here: You want them to know you and like you. Not only will they be better able to match you optimally, but also if they like you, they will be more willing to work hard for you. And you will also get much better and expanded service. This is just Psychology 101. When they like you, they want to introduce you to more candidates.

This works both ways. As they know that their other clients will like meeting you, which reflects well on them, they want to make you happy as well. When you have a strong relationship with these organizations, you will often find that your membership period will be extended for free and that you will receive many more introductions than you either contracted for or were stated to you. You will reap so many benefits from putting in the time with these people, including at least two in-person meetings.

CHAPTER 6

---■---

SEX: UNMASKED
AND UNHINGED

*"A clitoris is not an Italian sports car, and a penis
is a chocolate banana."*

SEX IS A LOADED, JUICY, AND VERY IMPORTANT TOPIC.
In this chapter, I have held nothing back, and I am direct, explicit,
and detailed. It is what everyone seems to want: honest and clear answers to the many questions we all have but don't usually have a safe
forum in which to ask or discuss them.

I have addressed as many of the tricky, complex, and dicey sexual issues that I can uncover. To the extent that some of my discussion is too explicit or crass for some of you, I apologize, but all of my
research tells me that a majority of divorced people strongly want to
know about these issues.

Let's start from the very beginning of the sexual journey in a
relationship.

So you really like her/him, the first date or two is behind you, and you think and hope it is time for the first kiss.

Men, how do you know if it is the right time, if she wants you to? Well, if she does, she has been sending you nonverbal signals all night, as you have to her. These signs are mostly subconscious, like light touches to your hands and arms, legs touching under the table, innuendo in the conversation, and leaning into and closer to you while you are chatting.

That said, I am a big believer in erring on the side of caution here. It is so much better to defer that first kiss and be sure about it and have it be strongly reciprocated. Be present and aware, and you will know. If you try for that first kiss, and she seems hesitant or not into it, then stop. Enjoy the rest of your evening without kissing. However, be sure to ask about the hesitancy at a comfortable time later in the date. If, on the other hand, she welcomes it and you click kissing-wise, enjoy that beautiful beginning phase of your sexuality together. Savor it, relax, and let it unfold. Remember that initially you might both be a little tentative, nervous, and restrained. Let it come to you. The kissing will only get better as you relax; get to know each other's mouths, lips, and tongues. Meld into each other. Great kissing is the engine of great sex. I believe this is an extremely important, essential component to a wonderful and lasting relationship.

Many people ask me: can a couple improve the kissing dynamic?

Yes, you can, within limits. If for some reason the basic interaction and the structural connection just don't work at all, then it is probably a lost cause (see Chapter 10 for the Apple computer and walk date!). Beyond that, you can improve the kissing a lot. Many people are nervous and tentative at first, so stay with it. Keep kissing, and don't be too ardent right away (that means, for you men, especially, don't stick your tongue into her mouth until you know she likes that and is comfortable with it at this stage of the relationship). Play a bit, do soft lip kisses, just a little bit of tongue; savor and play. As you both relax and get to know each other's kissing style and mouths, it will get better. At the same time, as with all things sexual, try not to be in your head too much. Enjoy the feelings and sensations as much as you can. This early kissing stage is such a pure, beautiful part of your relationship. Kiss for hours, if it feels right.

At the same time, if there are certain aspects of the kissing that don't seem quite right, talk about it after your kissing session is over. Ask the questions, tell each other what you liked and didn't like. As long as you always do it with soft, considerate kindness, you won't hurt each other's feelings, and you will get valuable answers.

Now, it's been a few dates, the kissing and touching have been awesome, and the next natural first question is should you wait for more involved sexuality if you think there is real potential? If you don't think there is real potential but the chemistry is great, then there is no <u>relationship</u> risk to having sex right away! There is the "clinging" risk of one person becoming attached, and of course, you have to address the STD, birth control, and abortion issues. You also need to try to be together at his/her place so you can control your time together and can decide when you want to leave.

But if you think there may be real potential, you want to seriously consider the timing of real intimacy, which I define as when the clothes come off, and you have either oral sex or sexual intercourse.

If you sense there is real potential, then waiting a reasonable amount of time has no downside if the connection is good. Waiting heightens the anticipation; the couple gets to know each other better, leading to more intimate and better first sex. And the emotional development keeps pace with the sexual activities, creating a more solid foundation on which to build. So wait.

What is a reasonable time period? I suggest five to seven dates or a few weeks. And again, talk about STDs, birth control, and abortion before you start having sex. That discussion, though it can enhance closeness and intimacy, is a romance killer if you are in bed at the time and are in the middle of it!

Allow the intimacy and sexual activity to evolve gradually before making love. After the first kiss, on the next date, have that first passionate make-out session, where you are pressing against each other, touching each other, but staying fully clothed. Next time, some limited clothing removal and intimate touching of breasts and genitals but no full clothing removal. Assuming all feels good and natural, then next time, get naked and explore each other's bodies. This could be the first oral sex of the relationship, a critically important issue. (More on that later.)

MAKING LOVE THE FIRST TIME

This is one of the most magical experiences of a new relationship, so savor and relish it. Set up a romantic situation, whether that's a romantic dinner at a restaurant or at home or a beautiful getaway (see my recommended getaway section in the back of the book). You might arrange a picnic with music and flowers, followed by a walk.

Put some time and effort into this because it is a special, one-time moment in your relationship. Show your partner that you really care. You'll share only one first time together, so make it memorable.

That first time you're making love, fully savor each moment. Don't rush anything. Kiss for a while, take off each other's clothes slowly and explore each other's bodies for a while before getting into heavy-duty sexuality. Spend the time to really get each other very turned on and wanting each other badly. You will know when it is the right time to make love. When that beautiful moment arrives, take your time. Enter her slowly and gradually. That first penetration is tantalizing for both of you and extremely erotic and exciting. Penetrate a bit farther and then withdraw, tease each other before getting into full lovemaking action. Savor every moment and be as present as you can.

Men, don't come too soon. Unless there is a health problem, time endurance in men is mostly a function of how long it has been since their last orgasm and how long they have been turned on without one since. So, men, take care of yourself the night before or that morning, and, women, be sensitive to how much making out and fondling are going on before the main act. Be attentive to your partner.

The first time you have oral sex or make love, it is often harder for women to come, so neither of you should make too much of that issue. Women seem to have more difficulty relaxing and getting out of their heads the first few times, so, men, don't make a big deal out of it. All that does is put pressure on her and increase the chances she will feel as though she needs to fake an orgasm to take the pressure off. Of course, it is always better if both of you come, but don't overly focus on this, especially the first time or two. You will have plenty of time to talk about it and to get to know each other's bodies.

After making love, men tend to fall asleep, but women want to cuddle and chat. This creates some real problems. Instead, try to do a little of both. Men, try to stay awake for a little while. And women need to understand that the hormones released during and after male orgasms cause sleep, so it's not their fault! Forgive men their post-coital nap. After their nap, men will be more likely to and surely more physically capable of making love again. So hopefully, you will have all night and the morning to cuddle and chat as well as to make love again.

ORAL SEX

This is usually the first really intimate sexual interaction, so it's very important. Over 70 percent of men consider oral sex the most pleasing and erotic of sexual acts. Though not as many women agree (studies show only 35 percent of women say that receiving oral sex is their favorite sexual activity), they too value it highly when done well. So men, learn to do it well! Learn to like it, love it, relish it. It is not rocket science. Your partner will show you what she likes with her moans and groans, the movement of her pelvis, or if you are lucky, with her erotic words of encouragement.

Giving Oral Sex to a Woman

For women, much more so than for men, oral sex is a means to an end, getting them going and turning them on a lot, making them wanting and ready for intercourse, which is most women's favorite sexual activity and the one that gives them the most frequent and best orgasms—toys notwithstanding!

With women, oral sex is more complicated because of their more complex anatomy and the fact that much of the female erogenous area is internal. One thing seems universal, and that is that women like to be warmed up; they like foreplay, caressing, and kissing, and all of that increases the likelihood of satisfying and orgasmic sex for women, quickies notwithstanding. (Quickies are addressed later.)

So men, warm them up. Kiss them; caress them for a while before touching the nether regions. Once down there, start slowly and gently; observe what she likes. Start licking very lightly and gently and observe. Explore all around on the outside of her labia, and only very gradually start penetrating with your tongue. Observe all the time. One of the tricks that you need to master is how to observe and innovate without being too much in your head and not in the moment. As usual, practice is the key. Practice most definitely makes perfect with sex, just as with most things in life.

Next, figure out whether she likes direct clitoral stimulation or not, and then you have to gauge how much pressure and what speed. You also need to discover whether she likes vaginal stimulation, whether she can have vaginal orgasms and G spot orgasms. Experiment and watch carefully what she responds to. If you pay attention, the signs will be there, and she will think you are a master. Later, ask her specifics about what she likes. My advice to men: If you want lots of oral sex, become great at giving it to your partner, and it will come back to you in spades.

One thing that can be challenging and rather enigmatic is the fact that what feels great to a woman on one given night might not be optimal on another. This is just a fact, and men need to embrace it. Though this scenario undoubtedly makes it more difficult to satisfy women, revel in the challenge and realize that it will make it that much more gratifying to <u>both</u> of you when you figure it out. You may need to vary the pressure, locations, speed, and direction and carefully observe how she reacts. Incidentally, though we are primarily discussing oral sex right now, the same applies to intercourse. Women's preferences for how hard, how quick, and so on, vary with intercourse as well.

One technique for oral sex that many women enjoy involves a combination of stimulation on and around the clitoris with the lips, combined with manual stimulation with two or three fingers in the vagina (depending on the size and preferences of your partner). Thrust in and out with the fingers (vary speed and force and observe what she likes), applying pressure to the front pelvic wall, where the vaginal orgasm or G spot location often is. Women who like this technique report that it can often lead to powerful and multiple orgasms, not to mention driving them crazy and desperately wanting you to make love to them.

Oral Sex Myths and Truths

There are four common statements about oral sex for both sexes that I would like to discuss:

1. Most men do not take any particular pleasure in coming all over a woman's face despite how this is depicted in many porno films.

2. Most men don't put a huge premium on coming inside a woman's mouth during oral sex. Coming with manual stimulation can be equally if not more satisfying when done

properly. Sometimes when a man is about to orgasm, he wants quite hard stimulation, and the saliva in the mouth can make it more difficult to apply sufficient pressure. In such situations, the final moments will be most pleasurable if done with manual stimulation or with a combination of oral and manual stimulation. Such preferences are important to convey because you don't want the woman doing things she doesn't particularly like, especially if it isn't important to you.

3. The myth that most women dislike giving oral sex. Several studies show that over 65 percent of women enjoy giving oral sex and get very turned on by it.

4. Men do think about sex all the time and do find receiving great oral sex to be a very attractive aspect of a relationship.

Giving Oral Sex to a Man

Giving oral sex to a man is in many ways much simpler and straightforward because the penis is obviously fully external and there are a limited number of techniques that can be performed and that men crave.

The technique of the mouth and tongue going up and over the rim of the penis, the most sensitive area and the one that creates the male orgasm, is the missionary position of oral sex. It is tried and true and loved.

Also men crave the technique of using a combination of both the mouth and hands to go up and down the shaft and the rim. It's very important to go all the way up and over the rim with both the mouth and the hands because this creates maximum and continuous friction in the critical regions. This will drive men crazy.

A less-known technique, but arguably the most erotic for men and the one that will get men to come whenever you want, is a combination of the mouth going up and down over the rim with the hands rotating around the rim at the same time. This creates extraordinary stimulation. While it's not an easy movement to master initially, with a little practice it becomes very manageable—like the game we played as kids, when you tapped your head up and down with one hand while rotating your other hand around your chest!

If at any point your sexual activity with your partner doesn't feel natural and good, stop and talk about it. Try several times again, and if it still doesn't work, talk some more and try again. If it still isn't working, it's a deal breaker. Every great romantic relationship has great sex, and it should come easily (pun intended). Great sex alone doesn't ensure a great relationship, but it is an essential component. Sex in the beginning of a relationship should be spectacular because human nature is such that the intensity and excitement of early sex will fade. If it doesn't start out strong, it will deteriorate to unacceptable and even harmful levels.

FAKING ORGASMS

Faking orgasms is such a bad idea and definitely undermines the relationship, yet it is rampant. Over 65 percent of all women admit that they have faked an orgasm at least once, so the chances are, men, that some of your women have faked orgasms with you. By definition, faking an orgasm is dishonest and especially harmful because it takes place during a time when the two of you should be most open, vulnerable, and honest with one another.

I understand why it happens: Women feel pressured from men to come, and they can't! So they fake an orgasm to take the pressure off. Men need to try not to put too much emphasis on women having an orgasm.

Rarely, men also will fake their orgasms when there isn't sufficient friction between the penis and vagina, and there isn't enough openness and trust to ask for oral or manual sex at that moment. Obviously, men would need to be wearing condoms to be able to hide the lack of semen when orgasms were faked. They fake it, pull out, remove the condoms, and dispose of them. Mission accomplished.

For those one-nighters or very fleeting relationships, if the sex turns out not to be good, I can actually understand and even accept faking an orgasm, but that is really the only close-to-acceptable scenario.

If you are in a relationship with a future potential, please try hard to talk these things out instead of faking an orgasm. You will never improve the sex by faking instead of talking. Tell your partner what you want. Your partner wants to know what you want, but not everything is best conveyed nonverbally.

PHONE SEX

This can be a very exciting and fun complement to your sexuality together. Be careful not to suggest it too early, as, generally speaking, quite a large percentage of people are not comfortable with it. Studies suggest that over 40 percent of the population have never had phone sex, and of those who have, over 35 percent say they don't like it. So as always, if you would like to have phone sex with your partner, check in first to see how she/he feels. If both of you like the idea, then go for it! It can be really fun if both of you are comfortable and can let go.

VIAGRA, CIALIS, ETC.

A certain percentage of even the healthy male population at times has some kind of erectile challenges. With the advent of Viagra and its class of drugs, men are offered a great solution to this problem. If there are any erectile challenges, these drugs should be seriously considered, with the advice of a doctor, of course. Most men do not experience any side effects of note, and most find the drugs to be extremely effective. Sexually, nothing is more embarrassing or disappointing for a man than to not be able to have or maintain an erection, so these drugs are a great savior for those with this issue. Also, today the stigma of needing to use these drugs has virtually gone away. It has become mainstream!

PREMATURE EJACULATION

This can also be extremely embarrassing to men, but there are tactics that they can use to minimize its likelihood. For most healthy men, the length of time they can go with stimulation before ejaculating is mostly a function of three factors: how long it has been since their last orgasm, how long they have been turned on that night, and how strong the current direct stimulation is. So men, if it has been a while and you think you might be having sex the next day, take care of business a couple of times the day before, and you will greatly minimize the chances of a premature ejaculation. Women, you need to be cognizant of how long you've been turning on the man and realize that the longer you do, the less time you will have for the real action! Finally, men, while you are having oral sex and intercourse, be mindful of how much direct stimulation you are receiving, and if need be, pull out or stop the stimulation for a moment. Stopping like that will buy you considerable extra time for active intercourse. Pay attention to each of your bodies and learn.

SEX AS THE RELATIONSHIP EVOLVES

The biggest challenge is how to keep sex exciting and stimulating. Try not to get into sexual routines in which the order and specific acts are always the same. Keep mixing up locations and positions, be spontaneous, have quickies sometimes, experiment with outfits and toys, **talk to each other** about wants and needs and fantasies, and make them all happen. Keep asking each other what feels good, what you both like. Remember to keep doing romantic things, like flowers and little treats. Make sure you do romantic getaways for weekends or a day. Changing surroundings does wonders for stimulating sexual drive.

If you feel the sexual connection slipping, talk to a couples counselor immediately (refer to Chapter 4). Though it is surely unconventional and rarely done, I find it imperative for all couples to go to couples counseling while things are still exciting in order to build trust and a strong foundation for your relationship well before problems arise. Even though your relationship is going great, you will be amazed at how helpful and useful the discussion with your couples counselor is. You will find things to discuss and work on even without overt problems, and the experience will only make you closer to each other.

So the minute anything deteriorates, go to your couples counselor, who now knows you and your relationship and is perfectly positioned to help you. Talking almost always makes things better and almost never makes them worse.

QUICKIES

Quickies are an important and often overlooked spice to a good relationship. Do them and keep doing them. By definition, they take very little time, but they will bond you. They will put a smile on your faces, and they will make you laugh a lot when you reflect on your exploits. Try this at home in all of the rooms, on tables, chairs, stairs, floors, and of course in the car! Elevators are exciting and daring—but well worth it. Don't overlook garages—yours and public ones. And explore remote public places, including the back of an empty movie theater. Just keep an open mind and go for it!

MIDDLE-OF-THE-NIGHT SEX

Some people just can't get into this, but men especially find this erotic—even more so if initiated by their partner. Over 70 percent of men ranked female-initiated middle-of-the-night sex as one of their top three most erotic experiences. So make it happen! It doesn't have to be every week, but it should be a regular and recurring activity if either of you really like it.

INITIATING

It is critically important to the health of a relationship that neither partner feels he/she is disproportionately the initiator. This undermines how the initiator feels in the relationship. It should average as close to 50/50 as possible. We all know how nice it is for the other person to initiate, so make sure you return the favor as much as possible.

"NOT IN THE MOOD"

Never utter that phrase. It is a deeply hurtful and highly rejecting act. It is sex, after all, so even if you are not in the mood, get over it and **never** reject your partner sexually.

Sex can be the most beautiful and gratifying part of a relationship, but unfortunately, it is often one of the most neglected. More than 75 percent of married couples report an unsatisfying sex life with their partners. Don't let this happen to your relationship. Sex connects you to your partner, it feels so good, and it helps make you happy. Make sex a top priority. Think about it, work on it.

MAKEUP SEX

Sex after making up following a fight or argument is universally recognized as more intense, more passionate, and more aggressive than usual. It is extremely gratifying, and you should indulge in it every time you make up! Not only does it feel so good, but makeup sex further secures the relationship, which has just undergone some degree of trauma from the fight. Be careful, however, not to seek conflict to create the makeup sex scenario. I know of several couples that have gotten into a cycle of fighting/making up/makeup sex routines. That does not lead to a healthy relationship.

BIRTH CONTROL AND PREGNANCY ISSUES

If you are using condoms, which no one likes but early on might make sense, make sure you put them on correctly! More than 90 percent of the time, condoms fail not because they broke during intercourse but because they weren't properly applied in the first place. Women, make it part of the sexual experience to put the condom on men in a teasing and sexy manner.

As for STDs, I recommend testing, though I believe testing without full trust doesn't really do it because without the trust it is only a backward-looking view. If you can establish the trust that neither of you has any STDs and that both of you will have only protected sex with each other until you become exclusive, then you can use the pill, an IUD, diaphragm, sponge, or other new inventions.

And you still must have the talk about pregnancy and what you will do if that happens. Abortion is an emotionally charged topic, and even those who are pro-choice in concept have a much harder time aborting their own pregnancies. Talk about it before you are in bed, as the STD and pregnancy discussion can be an erection killer.

BEING A GENTLEMAN

This is one of the 10 Commandments of Sex, Dating, and Relationships, covered in Chapter 11, but I wanted to mention it here too, as it truly is one of the few real aphrodisiacs! Despite all the women's liberation and equality progress, women still love being treated like ladies by gentlemen. It all adds up. So, men, remember to always open doors, stand at the table when they come and go, pull out their chairs for them, offer your jacket when they are cold, scoot over first when getting in a cab, push the revolving door for them, send flowers and chocolates periodically, and pick them up from their homes or offices for dates. These should be permanent actions and not just done in the beginning!

BEING A LADY

If you women like it when men are gentlemen, give them warm and positive feedback when they are. Let them know how much you like being treated as a lady. If men are not being as gentlemanly as you would like, tell them how much you like it when they are, and tell them what you like. Find a way to softly ask for what you want.

PENIS SIZE

Talk about a highly charged and frequently joked about issue! This wasn't easy to research, but I was extremely persistent and believe I have discovered the facts. So here is the truth about penis size:

- The average male penis is five and a quarter inches long when erect.
- Thickness is equally, if not more important to women than length.
- Too big is too big.

Women dislike too big more than too small. Most normal-sized women don't want a penis any larger than a maximum of seven to nine inches. Penises that are too large are painful for women and can actually be dangerous. I know one woman who had to go to the hospital on several occasions, as her husband had an eleven-inch penis and ruptured her. Men like to be able to thrust to full penetration, so a penis that is too large presents some real problems for men's sensations as well.

The fit between the penis and the vagina is the key for most women, and despite a wide variety in body sizes among women, there is a much narrower variation in vagina size. So, most men who are five to eight inches long and reasonably thick have nothing to be concerned about. What really matters is their technique, foreplay, giving attitude, awareness of their partner's needs, and so on.

***

Sex is such an important topic in post-divorce relationships. It is difficult to find a reliable and safe forum for sexual topics. I hope this chapter addressed the questions and issues you have on the topic.

In addition, you can find more information and helpful tips on my website: http://2ndchanceatromance.com. Or, if you want some specific help or advice, feel free to email me at **greatlifeafterdivorce@yahoo.com**.

CHAPTER 7

—■—

THE MANY PERSONALITIES YOU WILL ENCOUNTER

THOUGH STEREOTYPES CAN BE DANGEROUS, THEY CAN BE HELPFUL in recognizing who is sitting across from you on a date. Even better, they can help you filter out people before they are across from you, saving you time and frustration.

Accumulated from my 400+ dates during the past eight years, as well as in consultation with six life coaches and therapists, the following personality types may be encountered in your dating life. They apply to both men and women, though some of them tend to be more dominated by one or the other of the sexes.

Once you know about these types of people, you can be on the lookout for the telltale signs of the ones you don't find attractive. No one fits exactly into these categories; some people will have characteristics of more than one type, but your awareness of them will help you identify potential red flags or danger areas.

NEVER BEEN MARRIED, NO LONG-TERM RELATIONSHIPS, OVER 40, NO KIDS

Red flags all over this profile! Not that there can't be explanations, but you need to know them. Without good reasons, though, someone who fits this description most likely has some serious commitment and intimacy issues, as well as a risk of bitterness at not having had either a long-term relationship or children. They are often very hesitant to open up emotionally, but tend to have a strong sex drive. So this type of person is often quite receptive to friends-with-benefits status or has a relatively casual sexual philosophy. Proceed with extreme caution.

DIVORCED, NO KIDS, INDEPENDENT, OVER 40

More potential red flags! This person may have wanted kids and may not have come to terms with the issue, though Father Time may have resolved it. Many who have this profile are bitter about their situation and are not yet capable of having a healthy relationship. Additionally, many were screwed financially by their exes, so they are resentful of this and have to really scramble to make ends meet. This raises the risk of a strong financial motivation driving their relationship decisions, and this mentality can seriously cloud their judgment. Unfortunately, this difficult financial situation is commonplace among divorced women. Please be circumspect with this person.

DIVORCED, KIDS, 30S AND 40S

This profile is the best target profile if you want a healthy relationship and no more kids. They know what it means to be married, to be a parent, and to make a long-term commitment. They get it. Try to focus on the ones who did not have a divorce from hell and have a cordial relationship with their exes. The nightmare ex can wreak havoc with a new relationship and can be draining and exhausting to you both. The big issue for these people is their financial security. Many are struggling, and it can warp their judgment.

SINGLE, NEVER MARRIED, NO KIDS, 20S AND 30S

Obviously, this profile is very compelling because they have none of the marriage and kid baggage, and they're younger and often more attractive. On the other hand, they have less life experience and wisdom. They usually want children and marriage is a high priority. They are more open and freer about sex, with generally stronger libidos. Proceed accordingly.

UNCONVENTIONAL STRUCTURE SEEKERS: SEEKING AN ARRANGEMENT, NO STRINGS ATTACHED

There is a small but fast-growing group of people who don't want the conventional relationship model. Many have been married and have grown-up kids who are out of the house, and they want a person in their lives but without the usual connections. This group is looking for more of an arrangement where the two people spend a limited amount of time together, usually the man provides some limited financial support, and there are no strings attached other than being sexually safe. This is a way to more formally seek and achieve the friends-with-benefits arrangement, and there are sites explicitly for this out there. The best one is SeekingArrangement.com (http://seekingarrangement.com).

FINANCIALLY INDEPENDENT PEOPLE

Though a small group percentage-wise, this group offers an interesting contrast to the other stereotypes. It is amazing what an impact financial security has on people. This group is attractively independent and in no rush. They have the luxury of time and patience to find what they need. I have found them to be much more grounded and Zen. They are better able to be honest with themselves and with their prospective partners. Well worth seeking out these people.

PLAYERS

These people are going on many dates simultaneously, looking to have sex with as many as possible. They are not seeking intimacy or connection, other than sexual ones. Typically, they are very smooth and know how to treat people well, especially superficially, with good manners, plenty of money, a nice car, great clothes, dramatic homes, and a very comfortable and indulgent overall lifestyle. This type can do a lot of harm to the unsuspecting recipients, as they can come across as being very charming and very sincere. The way to identify these types is to hold off sexually for even a relatively limited amount of time, as they have no patience whatsoever.

SENSITIVE COMMUNICATORS

These types are very attractive, especially to women, since their sensitivity and engaging characteristics are more rare in men. They love to relate and to connect verbally, in a real way. Sex is important, as it is to most people, but not so much as an end, but rather more as a means to communicating and to connection. Women love these types of men. They are sensitive, aware, and evolved. The common concern here for women is whether they are masculine, assertive, and dominant enough.

SEX ADDICTS

These people are driven by sex and sex alone. In contrast to players, who are willing to do a lot to get their targets, sex addicts do not have the patience or the staying power (pun intended!) to wait it out and seduce their targets. They need it now and a lot of it. Surprisingly, there are a lot of these types of people out there. The key here, as with dealing with players, is to wait to have sex. They will just disappear.

GOOD FAMILY AND RELATIONSHIP PEOPLE

These people often represent the holy grail of relationships for many people. They are firmly committed to long-term, healthy relationships and are willing to put in the time and effort to achieve them.

They have had great relationships before and understand the upside and the beauty of great relationships. They are lovers of the opposite sex and appreciate them for what they are. They love kids, welcome kids of their significant others, and happily embrace the parent role. You will know them when you see them. They tend to be less sexual than the other types and perhaps less intoxicating and exciting. They won't cheat on you or hurt you with indiscretions or indulgences.

SERIAL DATERS

These people love dates one to five! They are charming and seductive and at first seem perfect. They want to have sex quickly, and you are very tempted. They know exactly what to do and what to say in those first few dates. They sweep you off your feet with their charm, charisma, and sensuality. So wait it out to see whether they are for real or just in it for the next notch on their dating belt.

WEALTHY, INDEPENDENT "NON-COMMITTERS"

These people are comparable to the financially independent types, except they are much less oriented to commitment in relationships. They want to play the field and are very hesitant to commit. They are having too much fun dabbling, and they love the early intrigue and mystery. They are seduced by that and are afraid of the daily monotony of long-term relationships. They are afraid of people coming after them for their money, and they don't know how to identify those intentions from genuine interest. They are leery of people seeking financial security from them.

WIDOWS AND WIDOWERS

Obviously, this scenario is tragic and traumatic, especially if the deaths were sudden and unexpected. As with divorce, if your date is widowed, he/she will need time to get over the trauma and readjust to life. Make sure that when you meet, at least one to two years has elapsed since they lost their mates.

IN THEIR 50S

This is a fascinating group of people, some of the most physically fit and emotionally mature people you will come across. Many of this group are self-assured, confident, emotionally evolved, sexually advanced, and adventurous. I strongly recommend that, for those of you for whom this age group can work, you take a very serious look.

***

Knowledge and awareness are critical tools in today's dating world. The ability to identify what traits you prefer, along with critical red flags and deal breakers, is one of the most important skills that you must develop to minimize wasting your time and to save yourself a lot of heartache. Use these personality types to your advantage (if they apply) and get clear about what you like and what you don't like so that your dating life is more of a joy.

CHAPTER 8

---■---

YOU ARE IN A RELATIONSHIP. NOW WHAT?

I T'S OFFICIAL. YOU CALL EACH OTHER YOUR BOYFRIEND AND girlfriend, you have agreed to be exclusive, and you have severed all singles-related activity! Congratulations!

So what are the best practices? How do you keep it exciting?

I believe that a great relationship will have a two- to three-year honeymoon period on its own momentum, often longer. Savor that wonderful time, and try to extend it as long as possible by being creative, giving each other enough space and time apart, and paying close attention to anything that annoys each other or anything that isn't quite right. Address these immediately, as I've found the greatest killer to the honeymoon period is allowing annoyances to grow into festering frustrations.

You can also do more definitive and conscious things to not only extend and prolong the honeymoon phase but also create a long-lasting great relationship. Here are a few proven suggestions:

1. Give each other time and space. Spend time apart on your own, with friends, and doing separate activities. This gives you the opportunity to miss the other person and lots of things to share when you are together again. And you'll find each other much more interesting. Appropriate time apart will strengthen a good relationship.

2. Try new activities together. It doesn't matter whether that's taking tango lessons or courses together, joining a tennis club, or playing bridge. New, stimulating activities are one of the keys to keeping things fresh. Go out with new friends together, have dinner parties, and keep your social life alive and well. Have larger parties occasionally as well, and encourage your friends to bring friends so you can continue to meet new people.

3. Have quite time together every day, no matter how busy you are. Make it a priority to talk every day, even a little, and to have sex as often as possible. Don't allow the outside world to infringe on these two activities. This is essential and critical. Simply do not allow days to pass when you don't spend one-on-one time with your partner.

4. Regularly share with your partner what characteristics, traits, and actions you really appreciate in her/him. You can't do this too much. I find that expressing your genuine appreciation of and gratitude for your partner is done much too

infrequently. It is so easy to do and has such a profound effect. Not only does this give wonderful feedback to your partner, but it also helps reinforce inside you all of the great qualities in your partner.

5. Go to a couples counselor—even before you have any real problems. As mentioned earlier, find a great one that fits the two of you, and establish a strong foundation with him/her. Once your counselor knows you, he/she will be ready to help when you do inevitably have an issue. That way, you have a great chance of nipping the issue in the bud early on. I know this may seem counterintuitive—and it surely is unconventional—but I have found it to work extremely well with the couples I have guided and in my own life as well. When you don't have any real issues, it is actually fun to chat together with a therapist. And you do end up working on things, which is so helpful, even if those issues haven't reached the stage of being real problems. The very act of going together to couples counseling fosters an open and communicative dynamic that is extremely positive for the relationship.

6. Avoid getting into ruts and automatic, repetitive actions devoid of thought and creativity. Never take your significant other for granted, and remind yourself of that every day. Savor and be present with yourself and with your partner every day. The flatness and lack of excitement that so many relationships display do not surface overnight. They evolve from a gradual decline that happens each day, bit by bit. So don't allow that to happen. Be conscious each day, appreciative, innovative, alive, and always doing new and different things together.

7. Address problems immediately. Honor the commandment (see Chapter 11) of never allowing anything to fester. Sit down with your partner and talk about it; go right away to your couples counselor and work together on it. Talking things out can make a huge difference. It may not cure the problem right away, but it always helps and begins the healing process. Avoid yelling and screaming because this is destructive and hurtful behavior. Avoid at all costs lashing out in anger and saying something hurtful that you can never take back. Work hard at this one.

KEEPING SEX ALIVE AND WELL

The importance of keeping sex vibrant, innovative, creative, and satisfying cannot be overstated. Variety is the spice of life, so you have to work hard at keeping sex varied. Mix up positions and locations. Dress up. Play out fantasies. Go away to new and fun getaway locations. Use toys. Talk about what each of you wants and hasn't tried. Tie each other up. Watch porn together. Go to a high-end sex shop together, explore, have fun, and buy a few things! Push your boundaries and get out of your comfort zone.

Arguably sex is the most important binder and connector in a relationship, and it must remain healthy. Unfortunately, a sagging sex life is one of the top reasons people stray in a relationship, according to many studies. People miss the excitement and intrigue of a new relationship, so please work hard on this. Your couples counselor can be very helpful on this topic. Counselors have seen the sex issue many, many times, so they generally have a long list of suggestions.

Whatever you do, don't ignore the warning signs, and do address them early. The moment you see or sense the sexual dynamic between the two of you starting to deteriorate, act immediately. The sooner you do, the easier it is to address. The longer you wait, the more entrenched the negative or repetitive activity becomes. If you observe that the sexual routine is becoming repetitive, immediately change **something**. Do it on the floor if you are always on the bed, do it in a chair in the kitchen, or do it on the Persian rug in the living room. Have a bunch of quickies in the car or in the back of an empty movie theater. Definitely go away, just the two of you, on a few romantic getaways (see my suggestions in the back of this book for exciting, romantic getaway locations). Grab each other in the middle of the day and go out for a romantic lunch, followed by a visit to a local hotel. Get a day room at a nice local hotel one weekend day; or do a spa day and a sex day together.

The most important thing is that together you change the routine before it gets to be a routine. Once your sex life becomes routine, it gets harder to break out of that habit. But you can, and it is so doable. Be ready and willing to work and to fight hard for your relationship. It is so worth it.

USE MASSAGE AS FOREPLAY

Massage is a wonderfully sensual and erotic activity. Use it! And while it's always a lovely idea to massage each other, it's also nice to bring in a professional to set the stage for you. The professional doesn't necessarily do anything naughty (unless you both want that), but can get you both in the mood. That way, neither of you have to work on the other, and you both get prepped!

INTRODUCING THE KIDS AND THE PARENTS

Introducing your significant other to your children and to the rest of your family is an important step. It should be considered carefully—but done very casually. Wait until the idea feels totally comfortable to both of you. Don't allow any pressure from your partner to influence your readiness. She/he shouldn't be pushing you in the first place, but I see this happen all the time. So be kind and understanding to your partner and tell her/him that you just aren't quite ready.

When you are ready to introduce your significant other to your kids or to your other family, it works best at some fun activity, ideally with other people around to make it easier on everyone. A barbecue, athletic event, or a small party is a good occasion. Let them feel each other out, talk to each other as they want. Don't force anything; let it develop organically. There is only so much that you can do. It's not unlike a science experiment—you put the ingredients into the test tube and then let them mix up on their own. Admittedly, this can be a nerve-racking time, especially when kids or family members do not get along with your significant other; this can become a major relationship problem. If that turns out to be the case, seek the help of your couples counselor immediately upon observing any conflict. Sometimes the perceived problem is just early jitters or nervousness, but if it is something more fundamental, work on it right away.

If there is a fundamental problem between your significant other and your kids or your parents, it can create a major wedge—with you caught in the middle. Especially when your kids are involved, such conflict can be extraordinarily stressful and debilitating.

If couples counseling doesn't help, you will have to decide whether the conflict is sufficiently problematic to warrant ending the relationship. When the children are still relatively young and have quite a few years at home before going away to college or entering the workforce, an ongoing conflict between your kids and your partner is especially hard. This situation will likely breed anger, frustration, and resentment and can destroy your relationship.

LIVING TOGETHER

Deciding to share a home together is a wonderfully exciting development in a relationship. It is a big deal—and a big change. First, think about the issue carefully and over time on your own before discussing it with your partner. Once you're clear, then discuss it together. As with all important decisions, it's never a good idea to rush. Take your time and sit with the idea. If it feels right, proceed. If there is a strong lingering doubt, wait and hold off for the time being. We'll cover more on this topic in Chapter 9.

LONG-TERM COMMITMENT

Making a long-term commitment to each other is obviously a concept that you need to evaluate and consider extremely seriously, as its implications and consequences are far-reaching for you, your kids, and your extended family.

The idea of a second marriage is very appealing to many, but consider it carefully. As we all know, it carries serious legal implications. Please know that prenuptial agreements are not ironclad. I have worked with several couples for which the prenup did not stand up. (I go into more detail in Chapter 9.) So this becomes a primary reason to consider not getting married. If you are not married, then your assets are not jeopardized, or at least much less so, if you decide to split up.

Of course, there is a wonderful additional psychological sense of commitment and a public reaffirmation that the act of marriage provides, and that is of real value and comfort. All I'm saying is that, especially the second or third time around, think carefully about the pros and cons of getting married. It is feasible to make a long-term commitment without actually getting married, so consider that possibility as well.

If you are going to have children the second time around, then I am much more supportive of marriage. It's well proven that having the same last name as their parents is healthy for the kids, and the marriage further protects the long-term financial security of the children.

Deciding to make a long-term commitment is an exciting and meaningful milestone. And while we all like the romantic ideal of marriage, you must also carefully consider the harsh realities. Believe it or not, second marriages have an even higher rate of divorce than do first marriages, currently at more than 60 percent. So buyer beware!

I have one slightly crazy idea, which some couples have really liked, and I'd like you to consider it, too. Think about making a long-term commitment to each other but, instead of getting married conventionally, get permanently engaged. You have formally committed to each other, and you can even have a religious ceremony and party without the legal component. For some, this has been a perfect way to make the commitment but avoid the legal risks of marriage. Food for thought.

BEING IN LOVE

What drives so many of us to pursue a relationship is that incredibly strong desire to be in love. Being in love is intoxicating, and we feel so happy when we are in love. It is, in many ways, like being on a drug. Though sustaining it is undoubtedly difficult, it is worth the search and the effort.

Being in love is the romantic equivalent of parental love. When in love, one becomes selfless and strongly desires to please a partner. I mention this because so many people have never been in love, and I believe it is worth seeking. Once you have experienced the feeling of being in love, you want it again, and you want it to be lasting. It is a very natural human desire.

KIDS

As mentioned earlier, this is a topic that you need to discuss early in your dating relationship. So by the time you are exploring your long-term relationship, you have already resolved the question of whether the two of you want more children, and if you stay together, whether you are going to have children together.

Nevertheless, this is a **huge** decision, with life-long implications for both of you. Make sure you are both completely comfortable with your decision. If you have both already had children, then at least you know exactly what you are getting yourselves into. If either of you has never had children, and you are planning on having a child together, I cannot recommend strongly enough that you discuss it extensively with a counselor. While children are a source of incredible joy and deep contentment, no single factor contributes more to the stress and strain on a relationship than a new child. Prepare yourself and your partner as best you can.

Also, if either of you brings children from a previous relationship into your new one, discuss in great detail each of your hopes and expectations of the other with regard to involvement with the children. Parenting style, values, and approach must also be discussed as much as possible throughout the relationship.

***

I hope this chapter will help you cement and strengthen that great relationship you have found together. It is a living, breathing creation that is constantly changing and needs daily attention, care, and commitment.

CHAPTER 9

THE EXCLUSIVITY DECISION, STDS, PREGNANCY AND ABORTION, THE MARRIAGE DECISION

WHEN THE TWO OF YOU FIRST MET, YOU WERE CASUALLY DATING several people, perhaps fooling around with one or two, but having no meaningful attachments or commitments. Then you met this current one, with whom you immediately wanted to spend more time. In the first few weeks of the new relationship, you still went out on a couple of first dates because your overall dating machine was still in full production mode and you still monitored the online sites. But over time, you unilaterally ended those casual dalliances, without even discussing it with your new interest.

Now enough time has passed with your new relationship that you are sleeping together (safely, of course), and the time has naturally come to address the exclusivity issue. Just the discussion itself and how your partner handles it—and how he/she reacts to these extremely important issues—can give you important insights, the same way first-date questions do.

The sexual exclusivity discussion, and eventually the decision, is an important turning point for your relationship. It sends your partner strong signals, so make sure you have thought it through and feel completely comfortable making this transition.

There are several components to exclusivity that must be addressed, sometimes at different times and during different relationship stages.

DISCUSSING SEXUAL EXCLUSIVITY AND SAFETY

I am a huge advocate of discussing STD and pregnancy issues before you are in bed together. In bed, this discussion is a romance killer. It feels less awkward if discussed well in advance. I advocate bringing this up as soon as you know you will start having more involved sexual activity than just fooling around. Have it ready in the back of your mind, and when sex naturally comes up in discussion, as it often does—**and** the feeling between the two of you at that moment is light and close—bring it up. Be direct and honest, as this is always best. Try to overcome any awkwardness and be caring and thoughtful, as you undoubtedly are.

As sex is broached in the conversation, say something like, "I am so enjoying the beginning of our sexuality together and slowly discovering each other, and I wanted to talk to you about some things when we aren't actually in bed. Are you comfortable discussing it now?" If there isn't any real hesitation on your partner's part, then proceed delicately. If your partner shows any serious hesitancy, table it for another time.

No one likes using condoms because of the reduced sensitivity and interruption required to put them on, but at times, they may be necessary and are the best short-term option. They represent a viable way to prevent both STDs and pregnancy. If women are willing to use birth control pills, the patch, the sponge, or even an IUD, then men may be able to avoid using condoms, but they then have to address the disease issue, because those other birth control methods do not afford any disease protection. Go online to do research on the most recent developments in contraceptive alternatives.

Obviously, it is important to discuss the disease issue. Hopefully neither of you has an STD. If either of you do, and it is transmissible and not curable, then you have some serious thinking and soul-searching to do. Can you live with the precautions necessary and the risk of getting the disease? In this situation, you owe it to your partner to decide quickly, and regardless of your decision, make sure to give strong positive feedback to your partner about her/his honesty about a very difficult issue.

If your partner is willing to use one of the non-condom birth control methods, you still need to discuss the STD issue. Many people ask their partners to get tested, and I support testing to be sure about the past, especially as it relates to some asymptomatic carrier-only diseases.

But testing is no help going forward because all it does is address the past. To have sex using birth control options other than condoms, you must truly trust your partner in the present and the future in order to be safe. If there isn't trust, then the test results of the past are meaningless. So, if you trust your partner, you can move forward with non-condom sex. If either of you don't trust the other, perhaps you shouldn't be having sex. (But if you do have sex, use condoms!)

In my discussions with many single men and women, I have been shocked at how many use a combination of the rhythm and pull-out method as their way of birth control. If women are extremely regular with their periods, the odds of the rhythm method working improves, but it is still a risky approach. Also, the pull-out-before-men-come method is especially risky, as the penis secretes considerable sperm well before ejaculation. I strongly advise against either of these two methods for birth control, especially if women are well within their optimal childbearing years. And obviously, these two methods don't address disease issues. Furthermore, pulling out can seriously reduce the pleasure of the orgasm for men. Unless continued stimulation is immediately applied as they pull out, the sudden change from active stimulation as they are having an orgasm to zero stimulation as the orgasm happens can be quite unpleasant. Many women I discussed this issue with were not aware of this, so make sure you discuss it!

DISCUSSING ABORTION

If you are having sexual intercourse, you must discuss the abortion issue. Only abstinence is a guarantee that women won't get pregnant.

Obviously, this is a critically important topic because it can forever change lives. Please talk with your partner what the two of you will do if a pregnancy should happen. And it should be the two of you in it together. Discuss whether an abortion is acceptable, or if you would keep the baby or give it up for adoption. This is tough stuff. Over the years I have seen even the strongest pro-choice advocates completely fold when it was their child, and many times they are unable to proceed with an abortion. So do some soul-searching to truly know what you would do under these circumstances and share your thoughts with your partner. Discuss the finances, how you might find a doctor, who you would tell, and so on. No one enjoys this unpleasant topic, but it is so important to make sure that you and your partner are on the same page. If not, figure out a way to get there.

HORMONAL ISSUES/MENOPAUSE

As people age, hormone production can fluctuate and falter. If you experience some seemingly inexplicable changes in energy levels, libido, headaches or migraines, sexual drive, frequency and capability, lubrication, etc., then it is worth having your hormone levels and production tested. Though stress reduction, exercise, and diet can have a positive impact, sometimes hormone treatments are the only significant solution.

Also, though menopause is a definitive hormone-related event, the physical consequences vary tremendously from woman to woman. The good news is that there is now a wealth of research and knowledge about this topic and many treatment options. My main point here is to not simply accept a deteriorated physical or psychological condition, but rather seek solutions.

OTHER EXCLUSIVITY ISSUES

These very important topics include each partner's agreed upon conduct with other partners. To many, this seems obvious and apparent, but believe me, it's worth discussing. You'd be amazed at the wide range of perceived acceptable behavior out there in a so-called exclusive relationship.

For example, a healthy exclusive relationship should address the issue of nonsexual social contact with the opposite sex, massages with happy endings, visits to strip clubs, use of professional call girls or men, acceptable behavior at bachelor and bachelorette parties, etc.

Are you surprised and shocked that these topics need to be discussed?

You have good reason to be because for many people, perhaps even most, these boundaries would be obvious, but the studies that have been done and the interviews that I have conducted indicate that more than 30 percent of men and more than 20 percent of women consider at least one of the above activities to be perfectly acceptable within an exclusive relationship! **So talk about them with your partner to avoid any misunderstandings!**

Less critical but also important is how you each feel about being a platonic date or companion for someone at a business function. These can be important business opportunities, but are you OK with your partner going on one of these? Think it through and discuss. As with most important human relationship issues, the key to anticipating and preventing problems is to talk about them ahead of time, if possible, but for sure immediately when they come up. **Never let any issue fester**.

Not allowing anything to fester is one of the 10 Commandments of Sex, Dating, and Relationships (see Chapter 11). These 10 commandments are so critical to the success of any relationship that I advocate that both partners in a relationship commit explicitly to each one.

DECIDING ON THE TIMING OF EXCLUSIVITY

I don't believe there are any hard-and-fast rules on the timing of when you start your exclusive relationship. However, I do believe strongly that you need to have this discussion. Assuming you are exclusive is an extremely dangerous assumption. If you start feeling that you want to be exclusive, bring it up with your partner, and make sure you define what exclusivity means to each of you.

And I suggest that you not sit with your exclusivity desire too long. Waiting falls under the "no festering rule," and you won't feel good thinking your partner is not being exclusive when you want him/her to be. Chances are that your partner is feeling exactly the same way you are, but you need to make sure.

LIVING TOGETHER

Obviously living together is a huge step and intensification along the exclusivity spectrum. And an extremely exciting one when done properly and at the right time.

There is no magic formula as to when it's the right time in a relationship to consider moving in together, but this is a very natural evolution in a healthy relationship. When it comes into your mind the first time, think about it, and then think about it a lot more.

Don't bring it up with your partner until you have thought about it at length and feel totally comfortable with the idea.

Once you're ready, discuss the idea with your partner. Though some initial trepidation is entirely normal and not necessarily a bad sign, once the two of you have decided to move in together, you should both feel exhilarated at the prospect.

If the two of you have decided to move in together, the first important decision is whether to get a new place or whether to move into one of your places. If possible, I strongly recommend getting a new place for the two of you to move into. A new place starts with a fresh slate and is completely neutral territory without any previous history or memories. Sometimes a new place isn't feasible, so in that case try to have a new beginning in the old place by buying some new furniture and art or getting new plates, cutlery, and glasses for the kitchen. Try to make it feel like a new place for the two of you.

Also, if possible, it is healthy if, in addition to the new joint place, you can keep your old place as well. It is helpful to have a place to go when you want alone time, something that is hard to create in a shared home.

Moving in together is a big deal. Do not take it lightly. It represents a major commitment to each other and starts to intertwine your lives together.

This is a beautiful new stage in a relationship when it is right, and a major stress creator when it is not. Do not ignore any signs of hesitation or stress if they manifest themselves as you contemplate this big change. If you have ongoing, serious reservations, wait and do not move in together. As I have said before and will reiterate many times, waiting is never a bad idea with these important steps. A great relationship will withstand the test of time.

MARRIAGE

The big "M" word! I began to explore this topic in Chapter 8, but it is such a loaded topic, I want to go into more detail.

Marriage is a big step for anyone, and for those who are divorced, the concept often comes with a lot of baggage. Nevertheless, marriage can be a wonderful choice for many couples, even the second or third time around, while for others it is an unnecessary legal complication.

Many of us still view marriage as the ultimate representation of a romantic relationship. Unfortunately, many people also view marriage in a fantasized and unrealistic manner, with hopes and expectations of 50 years or more of marital bliss. The truth is that fewer than 2 percent of marriages result in a 50-year blissful state. In fact, over 50 percent of first marriages end in divorce; over 60 percent of all second marriages end in divorce; and of those marriages that don't divorce, over 50 percent of those report not being happy in their marriages. So this means that over 75 percent of the people in marriages are not happy.

So why is the idea of marriage such an established norm in the face of catastrophic and ongoing failure?

That is a highly complex question beyond the scope of this book, but I wanted you to be aware of the realities of modern marriage. There is no doubt that being married often creates a deeper feeling of psychological commitment to the union, which often enhances security and comfort to both partners. Consider carefully the pros and cons of marriage for you, and definitely discuss it with your life coach and therapist. Explore whether and why you want to be married. If it is not absolutely necessary for you, especially the second time around with no new kids as part of the plan, consider not getting married. If the relationship ends and you are not married, the legal entanglements and complications are dramatically reduced.

And don't forget my creative solution (for some) I explored in Chapter 8: Get permanently engaged. You'll enjoy the commitment without the legal ramifications.

PROPOSING

If you are going to get engaged and married, give careful thought to the proposal and the ring. Most women love a romantic proposal and want a ring. Men, know her ring size and what kind of ring she would like, and have a ring when you propose.

And do the proposal at a special and memorable place. Come up with a romantic and fun setting in which to make the marriage proposal. Whether it's the first time or not, most women love a well-planned, romantic wedding proposal, and they will remember it for all of their lives. Many of the getaway spots that I describe in the back of the book are ideal places for a marriage proposal as well. This is important, so make it right.

PRENUPTIAL AGREEMENTS

Unfortunately, especially the second or third time around, prenuptial agreements are highly recommended. I say unfortunately because they are so unromantic, but the trauma of asset splits from a previous marriage makes a good argument for drawing up a prenup.

However, be properly warned: Even the best-constructed prenup agreement can be challenged and undermined. I have worked with several clients who had prenup agreements, but their spouses fought the agreements on the grounds that they were unfairly influenced by their spouse or were not properly represented. They were successful in sufficiently invalidating the prenup that an entirely new negotiation had to be held. So don't assume that having a prenup assures you of a clean financial separation should your relationship end. Far from it.

The foregoing decisions and discussions that confront you in your post-divorce dating life can be difficult ones. But, if you follow my advice and take the time to approach them with some forethought and care, it will serve you well down the road.

CHAPTER 10

■

HUMOROUS AND SURPRISINGLY TRUE DATING STORIES

JUST SO WE CAN ALL HAVE A FEW LAUGHS TOGETHER—AND TO help you realize that you are not alone in your occasional nightmare or shocking dates—I share with you the following absolutely true stories! Most of these are from my firsthand experiences with a few of my friends' experiences thrown in.

THE OVERLY ENTHUSIASTICALLY KEPT CONDOM

This guy was so excited to be able to have sex again after his divorce that he kept a condom in his wallet at all times so that, no matter where or when the occasion arose, he would be prepared. Well, after his separation and divorce, it took a while for him to have any sexual opportunities, and when the moment finally came, he excitedly opened the condom only to have it disintegrate from age in his hands! Very dejected, he was forced to run out to the nearest local drug store!

ONE-NIGHT-STAND SCARES

This man decided to have a couple of one-nighters to see how it felt, so he picked up an older woman at a nightclub. When they got into bed, she put her earrings on the night table, and then they had several hours of passionate sex. Later, after they had rested, she leaned over to the bedside table, and in one quick movement grabbed some restraints she must have surreptitiously placed there. Without asking his opinion, she deftly tied both his hands to the bedposts! For a few solid minutes, he was petrified, but thankfully she was just into a little tying up and released him after their next round of sex. The truth is, though, that you don't really know who is with you in bed in a one-nighter.

His other one-nighter gave him a scare of a different kind. He was at a dance club and picked up an artsy dancer, and they went back to her place. They started fooling around and ended up on the floor. As he entered her, she literally started screaming at the top of her lungs with such force that he could not keep his head next to hers. It was actually painful. And she didn't stop. She kept screaming so loudly that he had to end things very quickly.

REDEFINING HIGH MAINTENANCE AND AN ATTITUDE OF ENTITLEMENT

I had taken out this woman five or six times, and I had treated for everything each time. Then she invited me to one of those celebrity chef pop-up dinners, and I gladly accepted the invitation. When the day of the dinner came, about five hours before it was to start, my daughter got sick. I didn't feel comfortable leaving her with the nanny, so I called up my date and told her that, very regrettably, I would not be able to make it. She said she would try to get a friend to go. It turns out that she did find a friend and the two of them went. A few days later, the two of us got together at her house, and I brought some flowers for her. We ordered in some food, which I paid for, and hung out. All night she was subdued and aloof, so I asked her what was wrong. Here is her truly incredible answer: She said that I should have paid for the pop-up dinner that I wasn't able to attend (even though I had been originally invited to be her guest and even though she still went with a friend). She also said that two of the flowers that I had brought were rotten at the bottom of their stems!

It is still hard for me to believe the level of high maintenance and the total lack of appreciation that she displayed. I ask any of my readers to please email or call in any story that can top this one in this category! Needless to say, that was a deal breaker for me, and we never saw each other again. And she wonders why she is in her late 40s, having never been married and with no kids.

To add even more incredulity to this story, I realized afterward that I had met this woman a few years earlier and had already had a date from hell with her. The reason I hadn't recognized her was that she had changed her name and her looks. The first time we met, she was 20 minutes late and, when she arrived, was very irritated at me for picking a spot that was difficult to reach because of traffic. Imagine that, a place in Los Angeles that is a traffic challenge at 6:00 p.m.! She was so unapologetic about being late and so indignant that I politely told her immediately that we clearly were not a match and that I was leaving. She was taken aback, but I insisted and left. Can you believe that I went out with her again a few years later?

SQUIRTER STORY

Since I had never heard of women having squirting orgasms at the time I experienced my first one, I want to share this story so none of you have the kind of shock that I experienced. Incidentally, only 5 percent to 10 percent of all women have squirting orgasms, so it is quite rare.

I was dating this woman, and we had gone on several dates and decided to have a picnic at home at my place. We had a very romantic evening by the fire, with all kinds of delicious goodies. We started fooling around, and I began to give her oral sex for the first time. Everything was going great; she was clearly very into it and getting very turned on, and I could tell that she would come soon. All of a sudden, I was literally doused in a deluge of liquid. It was so much, I had a hard time breathing for a second or two. I was totally shocked and had no idea what had just happened. This is perfectly normal and serves nicely to let you know that she has had an orgasm, in contrast to those women for whom you aren't quite sure. So funny in retrospect, but not so funny at that very moment.

LEAVE IF YOUR DATE IS 20 MINUTES LATE

I have a rule based on common courtesy and respect that, if my date is 20 minutes late without calling, texting, or emailing, I leave. This has happened only once to me. I just believe that it is bad enough to be late at all, but to not even let the other person know is so rude that there is zero chance anything could work out between us. And besides, I don't want to be associated with someone like that.

FRIEND-WITH-BENEFITS RELATIONSHIP OVER A 27-YEAR PERIOD

I have a good friend who has had a friends-with-benefits relationship for more than 27 years! I know them both. They hooked up only when both of them were single, so they sometimes didn't see each other for extended stretches—but the relationship worked. When they first met as 20-somethings, they tried conventional dating, but they didn't click. Then a few months later, they got together for drinks and ended up back at her house and had torrid sex. That started the friends with benefits (FWB) that worked so well for so long. When they were both single, they would meet at her place and would be having sex in less than five minutes after he arrived. Occasionally, they met in public places, too. Generally FWB is a very difficult thing to pull off, as it must be balanced, but it is difficult to keep in balance because inevitably one of the two partners starts developing feelings for the other. These new feelings are often not reciprocated, and then the trouble starts. If you can find that rare partner who shares your perspective, an FWB relationship can be a very enjoyable and satisfying; it can nicely bridge the time between serious relationships. Needless to say, really good communication is, as always, especially critical in an FWB relationship.

ONE MAN AND THREE WOMEN

Almost all men fantasize about being with two women, but the truth is they should be fantasizing about being with three women. It works better.

This man attended one of his college's celebrations at the Waldorf Astoria in New York City. The party ended early, so he invited about 20 people over to his room at the nearby Parker Meridian Hotel. As the evening wore on, people started leaving, and eventually, he and four women were left. He could tell that it would be no ordinary night by the electricity and sensuality in the air, but he also knew that one of the women's presence was blocking the flow. So he very nicely told her that everyone was staying and that she was welcome to stay if she liked, but that otherwise she should leave. She left. The moment she walked out the door, all hell broke loose. The most amazing thing about that night was not the floor-to-ceiling mirrors, which he kept looking at incredulously, but rather seeing the women take to each other, two of them for the first time, and seeing how fully they gave themselves up to each other.

As I said, perhaps we men should fantasize about three women versus two, as the logistics favor three, enabling more one-on-one attention than a traditional threesome would provide!

Of course, the lesson in this fun story is the importance of being aware of the dynamics in a room and between people. If he had not sensed the block in the room, that evening would not have happened. It serves as a good lesson for many less dramatic, but often much more important situations. Pay attention to the nonverbal signs and messages in a room.

UNSALVAGEABLE KISSING STORY

A woman and I arranged to meet for our first date at the Apple Computer Store on 59th Street and Fifth Avenue in New York City at 11:00 p.m. on a Friday night because that was the only time we could make it work. From the store, we walked in Central Park for three hours! What a great first date. We got together the next day, and it was time for that first kiss. OMG! It so did not work that we both noticed it and actually had a chat about it. We even tried for another hour to make it work, but it just wouldn't. Such a shame, as we got along so well. And it wasn't that either of us weren't good kissers—just that the fit and the structure prevented it from working.

SPONTANEITY AND INNOVATION

We all know that keeping it fresh and mixing it up is so important in a maturing relationship. I mention this moment in a new relationship that was fantastic at the time, and that is an example of spontaneity and initiative that would spice up any relationship at any stage.

My girlfriend and I, at that point only together for a month or two, were at home going up the stairs when she grabbed me, pulled down my pants, and started giving me oral sex. The suddenness and impulsivity were incredibly erotic and exciting. It was so memorable, and I told her that many times.

Sadly, she never did that again despite my repetitive positive feedback. Nevertheless, it serves as a valuable lesson that spontaneous, out-of-the-box initiatives can be hugely memorable and impactful.

INADVERTENTLY JOINING A NUDIST SWINGER GROUP

In my earnest effort to embrace my new status as a divorced single, I reached out for new opportunities and to organizations to meet new people. When I received an invitation for a New Age love weekend,

I didn't suspect anything unusual, other than perhaps a more Zen modern-age version of the 60s movement. You can imagine my surprise during the welcome get-together when I realized that it was a group of nudist swingers! I made a quick exit, as I was surely not ready for that, and committed myself to doing more thorough research before trying new activities.

BEWARE IN VEGAS

My single male friend was in Vegas for a boys' weekend and was innocently playing at the craps table. As is not uncommon, an attractive woman started talking to him at the table and stayed for well over an hour, until he was finished playing. She was conservatively dressed and seemed exceptionally nice, so he invited her to his room. Once there, she offered to give him a massage, to which he happily agreed. As the massage progressed (he had only his underwear on), he thought he heard the clinking of chips but dismissed it. She got up once to go to the bathroom and then returned to the massage uneventfully. Ten minutes or so later, however, she again purportedly went to the bathroom, but this time he heard the front door open and close. Instantly, he realized he had been scammed, and he flew up from the bed and chased after her. Fortunately for him, the hotel corridors were long, and when he reached the elevator bank, she was still there. He demanded his chips back, enraged at himself for having been duped. At first she denied having taken them, but his anger and threat of calling security convinced her to give in. As they headed back to the room, she removed several thousand dollars worth of chips, which she had stealthily retrieved from his pants pocket. As if that weren't bad enough, she had also taken his wallet with all his credit cards, ID, and additional cash. He was so relieved and felt extremely lucky to have nipped it in the bud.

The lesson here, quite obviously, is that Vegas is full of scammers in all shapes and sizes, so be very, very careful. As with most things, if it seems too good to be true, it probably is!

BACKSEAT QUICKIE WITH A MARRIED WOMAN

One of my best friends was having a drink with a good woman friend of his, an attractive married woman in her 40s. He was single at the time, about six years post-divorce. On the way out, she tells him that she wants to get into his car because she has something private she wants to share with him. He was a bit puzzled but agreed. Once there, she tells him that she hasn't had sex with her husband in more than six months and that they are separating and would he please make love to her immediately. He was surprised, to say the least, but felt obligated to oblige! She dictated everything, including the duration she wanted, the pace, and the level of intensity. Once they were done, she thanked him profusely, gave him a big hug, and went on her way.

MISCOMMUNICATION CAN SOMETIMES BE A BLESSING

I had had two very nice dinners with an attractive 35-year-old woman. Admittedly, I was sensing a little excessive conservatism and reservedness from her, but I was hoping that it was just a little nervousness during the first couple of dates, which sometimes happens and then they often loosen up. After our second date, I invited her, by text, to a day in Laguna Beach at Montage for lunch, a massage in the spa, and a walk along the beach. To my amazement, she responded that it wasn't appropriate for us to have a massage together and that she, therefore, did not want to go. Wow! I made it very clear that the massages would be separate, but even if I hadn't, such a strong reaction to the idea of a couples massage showed me a lot about how conservative she was.

The capper came when I teased her about my last name. Many dating services discourage sharing last names for at least a few dates, as they want the two of you discovering each other yourselves—not from Google. My date had asked me for my last name on our second date, and I told her willingly. Apparently, she forgot it and asked for it again by text. I decided to play with her a bit and also to test how flexible she was, so I said that the dating agency had said not to share it (even though I had at dinner). She then responded that if I were not willing to give it to her, she couldn't go out with me again. What a blessing that this came out when it did. At least for me, this date was *way* too cautious and conservative for me. This incident illustrates one of those rare times when miscommunication turns out to be a real blessing.

KISSING BEFORE SEEING EACH OTHER

This is such a fun story! I was introduced to this woman through friends, but as it turned out I was traveling for a week before we could meet. So we started talking on the phone and spoke every day, culminating in an all-night chat for more than eight hours. Our connection and chemistry was so strong over the phone that I was compelled to make the following proposition for our first in-person encounter: I said that our week of talking was so unusual that we couldn't just meet for a normal first date. I suggested that we meet at the back of a movie theater and that she wait there for me; I would approach her and kiss her before actually seeing her. To my delight, she welcomed the idea, and we did it. It was very exciting and erotic, and our first kiss was wonderful. It was such a new experience to kiss someone without actually having seen her! We sat down and kissed some more for a while and then went out to lunch. We did end up dating for several months and are still friends. It was, without a doubt, the most creative and unusual first kiss that I have ever had.

MY FIRST AND ONLY WOMAN-INITIATED FIRST KISS

I am on a first date, and it is going extremely well. We are having drinks and appetizers, and at least two to three hours have passed. All the good signs are there—we are leaning in to each other, conversation is easy and flowing and intimate, she is touching my arm and being flirtatious, and neither of us seems at all concerned about time.

The conversation turns to her showing me some pictures on her iPhone, so I come around to her side of the table. Now I am very close to her. After showing me the pictures, she says to me, "I think it is time that we find out whether we have real chemistry or not," and with that she leans in and starts kissing me! WOW! I was very surprised and so turned on. Though usually I really like to be the initiator of the first kiss, I must say that under these circumstances, it was really fun and exciting. It didn't hurt that our kissing naturally worked immediately, but it was most assuredly enhanced by her wonderful assertiveness.

I wouldn't necessarily advise women to initiate the first kiss on a regular basis, but this wonderful story does show that sometimes it is the perfect thing to do. Judge the situations and the men you are with, and if you feel like it and it seems as though they are secure and adventurous, go for it!

***

These are just a few humorous and rather surprising true stories to add a little levity to your dating and relationship journey. Hopefully, when you experience a less-than-ideal dating experience or even one of those dates from hell, you will remember these stories and know that you are not alone and that at least a few "challenging" dates are part of the deal. Just think of it this way: the more difficult dates you have also means you will have more really great ones, too!

Please feel free to email me with your stories. You can submit your best (or worst) dating stories at my website: www.2ndchanceatromance.com, or email me at **greatlifeafterdivorce@yahoo.com**.

CHAPTER 11

■

THE 10 COMMANDMENTS OF SEX, DATING, AND RELATIONSHIPS

THIS CHAPTER INCORPORATES SOME OF THE MOST IMPORTANT must do's in the world of dating and relationships. I consider them to be truly absolutes, unequivocal, and indisputable. During more than eight years of dating, interviewing men and women, and reviewing these topics in detail with psychiatrists, psychologists, and life coaches, I have found these commandments to be essentially unanimous. Some of them have been mentioned in previous chapters, but this set of commandments gives you a quick reminder and reference guide to these most essential precepts. One cannot review these too often!

Keep them front of mind, and constantly renew your commitment to them. This practice will help tremendously, I promise you. Everyday life interferes and conspires against you, trying to prevent you from maintaining a vigilant adherence to these seemingly simple concepts. You may want to print them out and affix them to the refrigerator and your dresser. Make them part of your day-to-day life, like working out or brushing your teeth.

Here are your 10 Commandments of Sex, Dating, and Relationships, followed by a brief explanation:

1. Thou Shalt Not Allow Anything to Fester

    This is black and white. A small, relatively easy-to-resolve issue becomes a much bigger issue if allowed to fester. Then it becomes a huge issue when it festers. The issue gathers momentum, like a snowball running downhill on a slope. Resentment and anger build up, much energy is expended, and it boils up both subconsciously and consciously. Further, negative energy and emotion get triggered and then inappropriately expressed through some other, small annoyance, often in an explosive manner if allowed to fester too long. This is a huge issue, but one that you can easily avoid if you are honest with yourself.

2. Thou Shalt Not Date For At Least Six Months After a Separation or Breakup

    This is equally as clear-cut as #1, but it is one of the hardest commandments to adhere to. After the divorce, almost everyone is so keen to date, to have great sex again, and to have positive interactions after so many negative experiences in the relationship. But, again, this one is black and white.

    Allow yourself the time to heal, to do some serious personal development and work without the distractions of dating. In the big scheme of things, six months is nothing. Just believe the professionals who are virtually unanimous on this, and hold off! If you date too early, you deprive yourself of valuable healing and self-development time. And remember that dating too early is really a selfish act against the people you will date who might fall for you. You aren't ready for any real relationship, and all you will do is run away, disappointing and hurting those who are sincerely interested in you.

On the flip side, some people continue to avoid dating for an extended period of time after the divorce. You need to look into the reasons you are feeling this way and address them. This happens quite frequently and is usually driven by fear or insecurity. Often people in this situation are fearful of rejection after the divorce and do not want to feel vulnerable. While closing down and not being emotionally available keeps you safe, this also prevents you from having the chance to enjoy a close and intimate relationship.

3. Thou Shalt Always be Safe With Disease and Pregnancy Issues and Shalt Discuss these Issues with Prospective Sexual Partners

Very few people disagree with the concept of having the disease and pregnancy discussion and taking the proper precautions. It's when the couple does not talk about these issues ahead of time that things get bogged down. When they postpone the discussion until the heat of the moment, bad judgment is sure to follow, as their excitement encourages them to get take more risks.

So don't have this conversation during sex while you are in bed! Not only does the timing and location of being in bed increase the chances of a distracted conversation, but being in bed does not lend itself to an expanded, detailed talk. A good pregnancy and disease discussion can often last at least 30 to 60 minutes and can lead to a meaningful and philosophical discussion, especially if the topic of abortion is addressed, as it should be. So once you are clearly on the path to sexual intimacy, pick a relaxed time to bring up the topic and have the talk. It feels so clean, honest, and right to do it this way.

4. Thou Shalt Have a Specific Dating Plan and Strategy

It is imperative that you carefully read Chapter 1, Dating: How to Jump into the Pool and Not Sink, and seriously consider which of the various approaches fit for you; then regularly review how you are doing. Are you meeting enough high-quality candidates, or should you add another dating source? In today's world, with so many resources that weren't available when you were single the first time, please give time to considering everything I have described. Optimizing your chances of meeting that incredible partner takes time and energy and regular, honest self-appraisal and evaluation. And in the end, it is a numbers game—the more people you meet, the more likely you are to meet someone special who's right for you.

5. Thou Shalt Commit to Brutal Honesty, Openness, and Direct Communication in ALL Things

This is a tall order, arguably the most important of all the commandments and undoubtedly the most difficult to achieve. This commandment requires constant refreshing and recommitment because it is really hard to do. It seems easier to duck the difficult full truths or to just avoid discussing something sticky with your partner than to meet it head on. However, the moment you do this, you introduce a potential cancer into your relationship. Undisclosed important issues, even if your partner is never aware of them, undermine your bond with and trust of each other. Work against this happening with all your might. Keep reiterating your commitment to this with each other on a regular basis.

I suggest you sit down once a month with the sole and specific goal of talking about things you haven't shared and want to discuss. Even if certain issues seem small, bring them up, not only to honor this commandment but also to honor the commandment that Thou Shalt Not Allow Anything to Fester. Be devoted and assiduous about this; risk being overly so. The importance and difficulty of this commandment cannot be overstated. Use your therapist and life coach to help you with this challenge. Make openness and honesty a daily commitment, and reiterate to each other your total commitment.

6. Thou Shalt Not Go to Sleep Angry with Each Other

This is one of the easier commandments to uphold. Phew, that is a relief, because so many of the others are so difficult! Success in this one requires one of the partners in a relationship to be the mature one and to break the ice during an argument or disagreement. Just say that you are sorry and agree to disagree. Tell your partner that you love her/him, you don't want to go to sleep angry, and you need a hug before you go to sleep. Such a soft gesture does wonders. I'm not saying that it ends or resolves the conflict issue, but it surely takes the edge off. Adherence to Commandment #5 mandates that you continue the discussion and air out all of the issues' complexities and that you do it the next day to uphold Commandment #1. However, softening the dynamic and breaking the tension goes a long way to smoothing things over. It also gives you a chance to have mid-argument sex, which is always as good as, if not as great as, makeup sex!

7. Men, Thou Shalt Always Be a Gentleman to Women. Women, Thou Shalt Welcome and Encourage This Gentlemanly Behavior.

    This is tricky, because the best way for this to happen comes from parents who taught boys how to be gentlemen so that it became second nature to them. Unfortunately, many men were not taught this in their upbringing. One incentive to get you motivated is to understand that, despite our modern times and the liberation of women, most women love it when you are a gentleman. So if you were not taught to do these things when you were a child, you just need to teach and remind yourself.

    Basically, all you need to remember is:

    a. to open all doors for a woman;

    b. stand up when a woman joins or leaves a dining table;

    c. wait for all people to have their food before starting;

    d. insist on paying for at least the first two or three dates (after that it would be nice if the woman paid for something, even if it is a small gesture, to show her appreciation; see the section about paying in Chapter 1);

    e. help a woman take off and put on her coat;

    f. extend your hand when a woman gets out of a cab or car;

g. enter a cab first so a woman does not have to awkwardly scoot across the seat to make room for you, which is especially difficult in a skirt or dress;

h. push a revolving door for a woman when she enters;

i. offer to carry a woman's bags after shopping;

j. help a woman with her luggage in the security line at the airport and to put bags in the plane's overhead compartment;

k. offer your sunglasses to a woman on a sunny day if she forgot hers;

l. offer your sports jacket to a woman if she is cold; and

m. finally, offer to carry a woman if her high-heeled shoes are hurting her at the end of an evening (just kidding!).

An additional piece of advice on this one relates to your kids. Teach the boys from an early age to do all these things. That way, for them, it will become second nature and much easier to do. Keep reminding your sons a lot. This chivalrous, gentlemanly behavior is definitely not part of young people's social culture, so you have to work very hard to instill it. Believe me, it is worth it! Women really love it when men are true gentlemen—not just in the beginning but always.

8. Thou Shalt Give During Sex, Attending to Your Partner's Orgasms and Satisfaction, and Learn to Love Oral Sex and Teach ALL of Your Partners How to Do Oral Sex Spectacularly.

Hopefully this commandment comes naturally. It always feels good to give, but make sure you also give your partner plenty of space to be giving to you, too. After sex, talk about what he/she likes, what felt good, and so on. None of us are mind readers, so you need to ask. Not only does this discussion give you invaluable information, but it shows that you really care, not to mention that it upholds Commandment #5. (See more detailed information in Chapter 6.) For those of you who are not natural givers, this commandment may prove challenging. Work at it, as being an unselfish lover is an extremely attractive quality.

9. Women, Thou Shalt Not Take it Personally When Men Fall Asleep After Sex. Men, if Women Really Value Post-sex Cuddling, Thou Shalt Try Very Hard to Delay Your Sleep, at Least Some of the Time.

This commandment is self-explanatory and needs little discussion, other than to say that many of you women take men's falling asleep as personal affronts. But it's not. Post-sex sleep is mostly hormonally driven and is a strong sign that you have just given him great sex. Women, please don't take it personally. You can still have post-sex cuddling while he sleeps, and the pillow talk that you love so much can wait until later or in the morning. If he is a napper, then you can wake him up after 15 or 20 minutes and cuddle and chat to your heart's content. Also, important to both of you is the fact, proven by many studies, that a brief nap after sex reduces male recovery time for a second erection by 50 percent to 75 percent. That should be a big incentive for you women to give men a little post-sex snooze time.

10. Thou Shalt Not Fake Orgasms

This commandment is a bit sticky. Studies purport and interviews confirm that more than 50 percent of women and more than 15 percent of men have faked an orgasm at least once. We need to eliminate this tendency and recommit to Commandments #5 and #8. In the long run, faking orgasms does nothing but harm relationships. The only situation in which I can understand doing such a thing (though I still advise against it) is if you are in a clearly very short-term situation, like a one-night stand, and the sex isn't good and is taking too long. Otherwise, it is wholly destructive and undermines the openness and honesty in a relationship.

By the way, many of you women are probably wondering when and how men fake orgasms, as the evidence of a male orgasm is so external and observable. (And it's rarely an issue if men are healthy.) This does happen when, for whatever reasons but usually a combination of using a condom and a loose fit between the penis and vagina, a man does not experience sufficient friction and the orgasm is just taking too long and the sex no longer feels good. The man then fakes the orgasm to end it. His deception is usually not discovered, as he then quickly disposes of the empty condom, hiding the proof that he didn't have an orgasm.

Obviously, the much healthier alternative would be for a man to ask his partner to complete things through a hand job or oral sex. The issue of the fit being too loose or not having enough direct friction can be addressed, of course, through discussion and using alternative forms of birth control. If the relationship is important, men can also get a relatively simple and straightforward surgical procedure (see additional discussion in Chapter 6).

Both partners need to remember that putting pressure on women to have orgasms or multiple orgasms is unhealthy.

Many men feel that they haven't satisfied women properly if the women don't have orgasms. For some women, this may be true but not for all women and surely not every time they have sex. Have the discussion. Men need to find out how their partners feel about orgasms, what they want and need. Studies suggest that the main reason that women fake their orgasms is the pressure they feel from men to have orgasms. So men, ease up!

***

Honor your partners and relationships by committing to these critically important commandments. Reread and recommit to them on a regular basis, and your relationships will benefit immeasurably. Remember that adherence to these commandments has implications for your relationships far beyond their specifics, as so much is interrelated in relationships. Don't beat yourself up when you can't always uphold them all. Just keep at it and keep trying. Doing even one of these commandments will inevitably have a very positive impact on other aspects of your relationship.

PARTING THOUGHTS

I HOPE YOU HAVE FOUND THIS BOOK AN EASY AND FUN READ. EVEN more importantly, I hope it has been informative and valuable. I do know that if you follow the advice contained in this book, you will save yourself a tremendous amount of time, money, and frustration. The content has been proven in my work with divorcing couples and in my eight years of post-divorce dating and relationships, so I am 100 percent sure of the content's value.

The big question is, can you consistently apply the lessons, techniques, tips, and recommendations contained in this book? Please know that pursuing, finding, and maintaining a great and lasting relationship is no easy task. It is not smooth or uneventful, and, even in the best cases, it takes a lot of work and effort to optimize. But it is so worth the effort because attaining a meaningful relationship and finding a loving partner is truly one of the most profound joys in this life. So stay with it and fight the good fight.

And I am here to help you. As I've mentioned, I have mentored and guided many couples through extremely difficult divorces and breakups—and then into vibrant single lives. This has been so rewarding for me that I am now dedicating the major part of my life to this role. To that end, I am making myself available to all of my readers either by email or through our website, so feel free to contact me with comments, questions, or requests for help and direction.

And look for details about my upcoming specific couples work, seminars, Q&A sessions, and support groups around the country. I hope to see you soon at the one closest to you, and feel free to ask me the really tough questions! You can email me at: **greatlifeafterdivorce@yahoo.com** and find more resources and information at my website:

http://2ndchanceatromance.com

I wish you all the best of luck, good fortune, and a lot of fun and laughter along the way in your dating life and your search for a wonderful partner. Use the techniques and strategies in this book to help you greatly increase your chances of avoiding a lot of frustration, wasted time, and wasted money along the way as you find and keep that special love partner in your life.

RECOMMENDED BOOKS

The Five Love Languages - Gary Chapman

The Spiritual Divorce - Debbie Ford

All the Right Questions - Debbie Ford

The Way of the Superior Man - David Deida

Relationship Saboteurs - Randi Gunther

Getting the Love You Want - Harville Hendrix

Men Are From Mars, Women Are From Venus - John Gray

Why Men Love Bitches - Sherry Argov

He's Just Not That Into You - Greg Behrendt and Liz Tuccillo

Act Like a Lady, Think Like a Man - Steve Harvey

INDEX